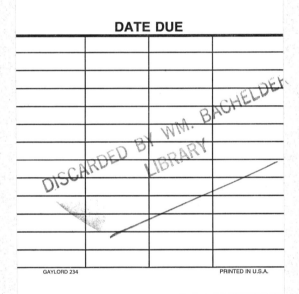

DATE DUE

GAYLORD 234   PRINTED IN U.S.A.

A DIFFERENT TIME, A DIFFERENT MAN

A DIFFERENT TIME, A DIFFERENT MAN

*How an Adroit New Hampshire Irishman Played a Key Role in
Financing World War II and Afterward Fought to Save the
United States Navy and Marine Corps*

THE STORY OF JOHN L. SULLIVAN,
ASSISTANT SECRETARY OF THE TREASURY FOR FDR
AND TRUMAN'S SECRETARY OF THE NAVY

STEPHEN CLARKSON

Peter E. Randall Publisher
Portsmouth, New Hampshire
2011

ISBN: 978-1-931807-98-2

Library of Congress Control Number: 2011938205

Published by:

Peter E. Randall Publisher
Box 4726
Portsmouth, NH 03802
www.perpublisher.com

Book design: Grace Peirce
www.nhmuse.com

Author's Note

A Different Time, A Different Man is a work of history for the lay reader. While it is based on historical record and refers to real events and actual historical figures, in certain cases I have set forth scenes and dialogue that, while based on my own best memory or that of others whom I interviewed, reflect in part my interpretations.

TO JOHN L., AND FOR HIS FAMILY

"Sullivan was a dynamo, a very able man, extremely capable."

—Admiral Robert L. Dennison, Naval Aide to
President Harry S. Truman, 1948–1953;
Supreme Allied Commander, Atlantic, 1960–1963

Contents

PART I

Democrat in a Republican State

1

Friendly Relationships on Both Sides of the Aisle

T he men were in the living room talking politics. Republicans all, they were in a jovial mood. A burst of laughter greeted the butler, who appeared silently to serve their late afternoon cocktails.

The host this evening in the large brick mansion on the New Hampshire coast was Alvan T. Fuller, owner of General Motors' most profitable dealership in New England and the former governor of Massachusetts. Fuller had gained national notoriety in 1927 when he declined clemency to the convicted killers Sacco and Vanzetti. His dear friend, the courtly Huntley Spaulding, chairman of a family fiberboard company in Rochester, New Hampshire, a prominent philanthropist, and previously governor of that state, was there as well. Fuller's two adult sons, Persh and Peter, provoked their father's criticisms of the current state of the nation. Sam Allen, scion of one of southern New Hampshire's wealthiest families, smiled at the young men's enthusiasm. The Reverend Theodore Ferris, Episcopal prefect of Boston's Trinity Church, listened attentively through the spirals of smoke from his curled pipe. George Bottomley, a surgeon at Massachusetts General Hospital in Boston and a staunch conservative, heartily joined in the excited expectations that Thomas Dewey of New York would soon return the Republican Party to the White House.

The conversations among the women in the adjoining parlor, which was lined with original paintings by Renoir, Monet, and Gainsborough, were more of family. Harriet Spaulding, Lydia Fuller Bottomley, and Persh's wife, Lee Fuller, exchanged exploits of children and grandchildren as a house guest of the senior Fullers, Connie Fields, who was then a senior at Goucher College, listened and observed politely. Viola Fuller, the governor's wife, was still out of the room directing the staff in preparations for dinner.

Momentarily Mrs. Fuller swished into the parlor and ushered the ladies into the living room with the men. A tall, striking woman with perfectly coiffed white hair, she was a grand dame of New England society. Smart and quick-witted, she was both a knowledgeable opera buff and a fine singer in her own right. Anxious that the dinner be a happy and successful affair, she struck right to a concern that had been bothering her.

"Listen up, all. The Sullivans will be here any minute. I don't want to hear a peep about the upcoming election at the table. Everyone knows Dewey is going to win, and that is undoubtedly weighing on John L. He's probably been working hard for Truman. We must not embarrass him." She directed her gaze in particular at her irreverent son Persh and knew he wasn't paying attention, but she did not see Persh wink at his younger brother, who returned a smile.

Shortly, Governor Fuller was called to answer the door to welcome his Democratic guest of honor from Washington, John L. Sullivan, the secretary of the Navy. He greeted his good friend warmly. They had been golfing pals for years. Fuller had great respect for Sullivan's judgment and enjoyed getting his insider reports from Washington. Neither man let political differences interfere with their friendship. Fuller kissed Sullivan's wife, Priscilla, on the cheek and led his new guests back to greet the earlier arrivals.

After quick introductions and light standing chatter, Mrs. Fuller directed everyone into the spacious dining room where a large glass chandelier hung over an oval mahogany table perfectly set with shining silver and crystal. An oriental rug of orange, yellow, and green hues spread over the entire floor. Mrs. Fuller seated the Sullivans in the center of the table with their backs to a full-wall mural of a New England harvest scene. This gave them a view through a broad picture window across a lawn stretching down almost two hundred yards to the rock barrier overhanging the Atlantic. Seven miles offshore the Isles of Shoals clung to the last rays of sunlight. The evening was clear but already cool, with only a hint of winter's lashing storms soon to come.

Mrs. Fuller sat herself with her back to the window as the first course of lobster stew was served.

The gathering was not more than three spoonfuls into their stew when young Persh's enthusiasm overcame his manners: "It sure looks like Dewey is a cinch to win. New England, New York, and Pennsylvania are solid, and the reports from California are very positive. Warren will help there. Also, Illinois and Ohio are strong. That should do it. The Republicans will be back in control."

Shock and silence met Persh's impertinence. In the pause all eyes turned to Sullivan, who carefully scanned around the table, looking each person square in the eye. As he turned back to his stew, he said quietly and matter-of-factly, "Not going to happen, folks. It just isn't going to happen."

Following another minute of dead silence, Mrs. Fuller turned the conversation to other topics, and the meal continued in a civilized manner. But after the Sullivans had left, the others rationalized and consoled themselves—"Of course he has to say that."

2

New Hampshire Nurturing

*T*hroughout his life, John Lawrence Sullivan was a devoted New Hampshire man. He was born and raised in Manchester and practiced law there. He managed several political campaigns and ran for governor twice. Over the years he became a respected political operative both in New Hampshire and nationally. He always kept his domicile in New Hampshire, although he continued to reside in Washington in the winter months after his government service. During the summers he and his family stayed much of the time at their other home on the coast, at Little Boars Head in North Hampton, New Hampshire, next to Rye Beach.

At the time Sullivan was born, on June 16, 1899, the United States was basking in a postbellum period of prosperity and national self-confidence. Republican President William McKinley, Jr., who had defeated William Jennings Bryan in the election of 1896, was a supporter of business combinations, consolidations, trusts, and protective tariffs who pushed to make American companies leaders in world markets. To facilitate the opening of new foreign markets he had annexed the formerly Spanish colonies of Puerto Rico, the Philippines, and Guam, established Cuba as a protectorate, and presided over the annexation of Hawaii. When Spain's resistance and its atrocities enflamed the American public and led Congress to declare war on Spain, which became known as the Spanish-American War, the Navy and Teddy Roosevelt's Rough Riders successfully consummated what Secretary of State

John Hay later called "a splendid little war" in just a hundred and thirteen days. Spain agreed to the United States' terms in the Treaty of Paris. Gold was discovered in Nome, Alaska.

The total U.S. population, of just over seventy-six million people, was enjoying low prices. The average home cost was $5,321 and an automobile's average cost was $843. A postage stamp was still 2 cents and a gallon of gas was 9 cents. Milk was 11 cents a half gallon and a dozen eggs cost 5 cents. The average annual income was $633.

Manchester, New Hampshire, was itself experiencing good times. By 1899 a city of almost fifty-seven thousand people, it had a unique and fascinating history reaching back to the prerevolutionary era.

The Pennacook Indians occupied the area before the white settlers came. They were attracted to the spot in the wilderness that they named Namoskeag—"good fishing place"—where there was a robust waterfall. That label survives in the name of the Amoskeag Falls on the Merrimack River, which rises to the north at the confluence of the Pemigewasset and Winnipesaukee rivers and flows southward into Massachusetts and then northeast to its mouth on the Atlantic at Newburyport. It is the second-largest river in New England.

Originally settled in 1722, the town was chartered as Derryfield in 1751. Derryfield's most famous resident was Colonel John Stark, who fought with distinction at Bunker Hill and was the hero of the battle of Bennington, Vermont, in 1777, the first significant American victory against England's redcoats. After the war, for a ceremony commemorating the success at Bennington, he coined what became the state's motto—"Live Free or Die."

In 1810 the town was renamed after Manchester, England, as the city's fathers envisioned and took steps to create a great industrial center. The transforming moment in that endeavor came in 1831 when a group of Massachusetts entrepreneurs acquired an existing cotton-spinning mill on the west side of the river and established the Amoskeag Manufacturing Company. That company over the course of the following century would turn the town into a factory-city.

The company purchased a large tract of land on the eastern side of the river and laid out, planned, and controlled the entirely new city. Elm Street, a broad hundred-foot-wide thoroughfare running north and south parallel to the river, was the centerpiece. New mills were constructed between Elm and the river. Boarding-houses, referred to as "corporations," were built along upper Elm to house young women working in the mills. The corporations were locked at ten in the evening, the women were required to attend church, and alcohol was forbidden. Land sales in the new city were strictly controlled. Amoskeag encouraged other privately held businesses to open, including shoe factories, a cigar manu-facturer, shops, movie houses, and dance halls. The company also controlled the city's aldermen and police force.

The company's absentee management in Boston attempted to assuage dissatisfaction among the workers and other populace by appointing an on-site "agent" to run the mills and all other aspects of its operations. The first two agents were Ezekiel Straw and his son Herman. The latter was particularly effective, a sym-pathetic soul who made a point of mingling with the workers and earning their support and devotion.

The makeup of the work force soon began to change. A heavy influx of Irish families occurred from 1850 to 1870. German, Swedish, and Scottish immigrants also came. Large numbers of French Canadians followed in the last quarter of the century. By 1900 they were joined by Greeks and Poles in smaller numbers. The city remained bilingual, its residents speaking either English and French, or both, well into the twentieth century.

Republican and Democratic political parties emerged and attacked each other vigorously.

By the turn of the century when John Sullivan arrived, the Amoskeag company had created the largest cotton mill in the world, stretching for one and a third miles along the Merrimack in thirty massive main buildings, all made from the same distinctive deep-red bricks.

* * *

John was very close to his father, Patrick, whom he admired greatly and who was the source of John's lifetime inspiration and drive. Patrick Sullivan's parents, John D. Sullivan and Julia Sullivan, were both from Ireland, apparently County Kerry. John D., the son of Timothy and Elizabeth Sullivan, was born in 1829. Julia was born in the year 1836 to Michael and Bridget Sullivan. They may well have been cousins and been put on a ship together in about 1848 by their respective parents so that they would have a chance to survive the ravages of the Potato Famine. The conditions of passenger on the ships coming to the United States from Ireland were appalling. The passengers had no food unless they brought it on board themselves, and the fares of young passengers such as the Sullivans were prepaid by their parents, so the ships' captains did not care whether their "cargo" made it or not. The death rate on these "coffin ships" was 15 percent, said to be higher than on many of the slave ships from Africa. The year 1847 was so terrible in this respect that it became known as "Bloody '47."

Entering the United States at the port of Boston, the Sullivans first went to Cambridge, Massachusetts, where they were married on June 29, 1865, at St. Paul's Church. Later they moved to Nashua, New Hampshire. Julia worked as a housekeeper; John D.'s occupation was described as "trader." They had two children, Patrick Henry, born December 29, 1866, and Mary, born in 1868. The father, John D., died in 1869, and their mother carried on industriously as a housekeeper and in a factory to feed her children and, pursuant to her husband's dying request, to "Give the children an education."

Somewhere in the Sullivan DNA there was intelligence and ambition. Mary stayed with her mother, and there is no evidence that she married, and Patrick supported himself with odd jobs before and after school. He graduated from Nashua High School at age sixteen in 1883. After high school he worked as a bookkeeper, and began studying law in the office of Captain H. B. Atherton of Nashua while also teaching in the public high school, clerking in a clothing store, and doing some newspaper work. He graduated from Boston University Law School in 1890 after friends who worked for the Boston and Maine Railroad allowed him to commute to Boston by riding free in the caboose attached to freight trains. Admitted to the New Hampshire Bar that same year, he began his law practice in Manchester in 1891 with another lawyer named Broderick. He also manufactured cigars, which he sold in a tobacco store that he ran. He was active in both the Knights of Columbus and the Democratic Party, and became a member of the New Hampshire House of Representatives in 1893. He was solicitor for Hillsborough County from 1894 until 1905, "declining farther election which he might have had notwithstanding the strong adverse political majority in the county."

Patrick married Ellen Harrington on June 15, 1898. Patrick and "Nellie" lived at 96 Webster Street, where his mother joined him after his father died, and also at 357 Walnut Street. His law office was first at 20 Hanover Street and later in the Amoskeag Bank building. He ran for the United States Congress in a special election from the 5th New Hampshire District in 1917, receiving a tremendous majority in Manchester but losing the overall district, which included surrounding Protestant towns, by just fourteen hundred votes in a bitter anti-Catholic race. Notwithstanding this political loss, Patrick developed a successful law practice, counting Frank Knox, publisher of the *Manchester Leader* newspaper (later the *Manchester Union-Leader*), as one of his clients.

Both in his law practice and in politics, one of Patrick's shrewd strengths was his ability to connect in business and socially with the WASP hierarchy that dominated the region. In this respect, he courted and won the friendship and support of the state's movers and shakers, including businessmen Norwin Bean and John Shontell.

Patrick and Nellie's first son, John L., the subject of this exploration, attended Webster Street Grammar School and the city's Central High School, graduating in 1917. A younger brother, Robert, was born on March 19, 1902, but died of meningitis on April 5, 1905. Robert's death was horrible and traumatic for young John, who became fearful of hospitals and people who were sick, and although he was warm and friendly, he would not even visit friends when they were in hospitals.

At an early age John developed an excellent singing voice as he also learned to play the piano. He sang in the choir at St. Joseph's Cathedral in Manchester. He was an all-around talented young man who was the brightest star as a youth in high school.

In 1917 Sullivan entered Dartmouth College in Hanover, New Hampshire, beginning the strongest and longest affection of his life for any institution. The man and the college fitted each other perfectly. He was naturally engaging, and his piano playing and rich bass singing voice added to his popularity at Chi Phi parties. His Irish affinity for making friends and remembering names and faces was becoming broadly recognized and appreciated. He also earned a reputation there as a fine debater. He once engaged in an intercollegiate debate against Brown University on whose team was a young man named Thomas G. Corcoran, later to become renowned as "Tommy the Cork," one of Franklin Delano Roosevelt's "Brain Trust." Sullivan's team was defeated by Corcoran's team. In the 1930s Sullivan sought help from the Reconstruction Finance Corporation, whose counsel was none other than "the Cork." When John L. entered the room to plead his client's case, Corcoran immediately remembered his old adversary and quipped, "Why in the world should I help you?" Sullivan replied, "Because my client needs help and is entitled under the law." After the facts were reviewed, Sullivan, to Corcoran's credit, prevailed.

He left Dartmouth in September 1918 to join the Navy as an ordinary seaman. He said years later that, "In World War I, I was anxious to get into Marine or Naval aviation, but you had to be twenty-one, and I had not reached that age and I wanted to be in a service where I would be contributing something and yet from which I could transfer to Naval or Marine aviation in the event that the rule was relaxed." He spent three months at a Navy flight training school at Yale before the war ended. He was released from active duty as an ordinary second class able seaman on December 23, 1918, and was discharged on September 30, 1921. His fascination with and devotion to the Navy would never flag.

Sullivan returned to Dartmouth in the fall of 1919 and proceeded to organize the first Democratic Club in the history of the school. He later recalled that, "We had eight members. The Republicans, I guess, had over one thousand, but we had fun." He was later elected "Mayor of Hanover," a mythical office that he fabricated. It is recorded that "campaigning about town in a rented coach behind an elegant pair of livery stable steeds while attired dazzlingly in a frock coat and top hat, he lined up the votes of his green sweatered constituents in landslide fashion." In his final two years at the college he sang in the choir and was a member of the Dramatic Association, the Players, the Arts Society, and the Forensic Union. He participated in several musical productions.

He graduated from Dartmouth in 1921, entered Harvard Law School that fall, and received his LL.B. degree there in 1924 at age twenty-five. While studying in Cambridge, he sang in the chorus when the Metropolitan Opera came to Boston. Having passed the New Hampshire Bar in 1923 even before graduation, he immediately joined his father's law firm, Sullivan and White, where he studied and emulated his father's personal and political style, cultivating strong relationships outside the narrow Irish Catholic and Democratic Party communities. Five years later, in 1929, he became county solicitor for Hillsborough County, the post formerly held by his father, which position he held until 1933. He became a name partner in the firm of Sullivan and Sullivan in 1930 and then sole owner when his father died on September 16, 1931.

The Manchester that John Sullivan returned to after college and law school was becoming quite different from the thriving city he was born into at the turn of the century.

In the first two decades of the 1900s, the city had made great strides in the area of cultural development, due in no small part to the many and varied contributions of the Frank Carpenter family. In 1900 the Manchester Institute of Arts and Sciences was opened. The beautiful Blood Memorial Parish House, the Historic Association building, the Hill House home of the local YWCA, the Carpenter Memorial Library, and the Currier Gallery of Art were additional manifestations of this evolution.

World War I sidetracked these strides, but the industrial mobilization of that effort filled the coffers of the Amoskeag company to record levels. Building continued thereafter: a new Queen City Bridge was completed in 1923, and the Manchester Water Works, two new high school buildings, a Boys' Club camp, and the Manchester Country Club clubhouse followed shortly thereafter.

But signs of economic trouble were emerging. After the war, industrial demobilization immediately followed, and the Amoskeag company began to decline. High labor costs, competition from southern mills, and antiquated machinery accelerated the trend. The company cut wages, employees, and output. The city experienced a demoralization, and many workers left.

The United Textile Workers of America appeared in the mills in 1917 and organized the company's first strike in 1919. It was short and ineffective, but in 1922 the company's announcement of a simultaneous increase in workers' hours and a 20 percent wage cut brought the strikers out again. The strike lasted for nine months, resulting only in union acceptance of the company's terms and the establishment of a company union designed to thwart the UTW. While it appeared to be victorious, the company would never recover.

There are no records reflecting how these adverse economic events affected the Sullivans' law practice, but it is probable that, given both Patrick and John's connections in the New Hampshire business community, Manchester's hard times had at most only a small effect on their successful law practice.

Patrick's early death in 1931 (John's mother lived until 1951) was a devastating loss that focused John L.'s attention on his life's direction and galvanized his ambitions.

John was determined to marry well, both socially and financially, and in 1932 he did. He had begun dating Priscilla Carpenter Manning, a 1932 graduate of Vassar College, while she was still an undergraduate there. Priscilla was a pretty and intelligent young woman whose wealth and family roots reached back to colonial New England. William Manning, of Saxon stock, and his family arrived in Boston from England in 1632 and his son settled in Billerica, Massachusetts, in 1666. The house where the son and his family lived, now a Chinese restaurant, still stands. Four generations later, Joseph Cogswell Manning, born in 1812 in Lancaster, Massachusetts, and his wife, Rebecca Livermore, and their nine children moved to Baltimore, Maryland. One of their sons was Captain Charles H. Manning, a graduate of the U.S. Naval Academy who later taught there from 1874 to 1879. He then moved to Manchester, New Hampshire, where he became an engineer and general superintendent for the Amoskeag Manufacturing Company. Captain Manning was famous for inventing the larger boilers used in the Amoskeag textile mills in Manchester.

Captain Manning's son, Charles Bartlett Manning, in turn married Mary Carpenter, daughter of Frank and Elenora Blood Carpenter. The Carpenter family had arrived in America in 1634, disembarking the ship *Beavis* at Cambridge, Massachusetts. In the early 1700s, the family found their way to Chichester, New Hampshire, a small town twenty miles north-northeast of Manchester, where the male heads of the family were Congregational ministers for several generations. Just prior to the Civil War, their descendant Frank P. Carpenter opened a grain business in Manchester. Later he founded the Amoskeag Paper Company and was a city magnate in banking and real estate.

Mary Carpenter Manning's maternal grandfather was Aretas Blood, who came to the city shortly after its incorporation and founded the Manchester Locomotive Works, a major industry in the area. Blood also served on the board of directors of the Boston and Maine Railroad.

Mary Carpenter Manning was widowed in 1924 when her husband and two brothers were hit and killed by Henry Ford's private railroad train in the state's "north country." Following her husband's death, Mrs. Manning continued to dedicate her life and wealth to community service. In addition to anonymously assisting thousands of individuals and families in need, she was the driving force in public philanthropy in Manchester for decades. An inquisitive, spirited, and progressive personality, she was active in numerous organizations, including the Manchester and national Community Chests (which later became United Way), the YWCA, the National Women's Committee for Mobilization of Human Needs during the Depression, the Women's Aid Home, the Carpenter Library, the Currier Gallery of Art, and the United Service Organizations. On two occasions she received awards for distinguished service to the state, and she taught Sunday School at the Franklin Street School for twenty-five years. She was a tour de force both without and within the family.

Priscilla Manning, the daughter of Charles Bartlett and Mary Carpenter Manning, was born on June 4, 1911. While Priscilla was an undergraduate at Vassar she yearned to become a physicist, but her strong-willed mother had talked her out of that goal, and Priscilla had majored in child psychology instead.

When Priscilla and John Sullivan met, the relationship immediately became an attraction of opposites. John was outgoing and gregarious; she was a shy and quiet young lady. Sullivan's quick wit made her laugh for hours. A college friend of Priscilla's remembered meeting John and exclaiming *"Erin go Bragh!"* which she had practiced beforehand. Sullivan "rendered [her] completely speechless by shooting back, *'E pluribus unum.'"* She also recalled John zipping about the campus in Priscilla's light-colored Franklin.

Even though the Mannings were established New England Protestants, Mary Manning saw Catholic John Sullivan as a good catch for her daughter and urged Priscilla to encourage John. Priscilla did, and the two were married in Manchester on December 28, 1932, six months after she graduated from college. She was just twenty-one, twelve years younger than her new husband.

When he finished law school, Sullivan had continued to live with his parents at the corner of Webster and Elm streets. After his marriage he and Priscilla moved into a house at 1330 Union Street, well north of the settled part of Manchester, on twenty acres of hillside pasture with a view of the Uncanoonuc Mountains. Both homes were a quick walk and trolley ride from Sullivan's office on the seventh floor of the Amoskeag Bank building at 875 Elm.

During their courting and their first years of marriage, John and Priscilla were often seen skiing and bicycling in the area. They also liked to skate and hike together.

In his early years back in Manchester, Sullivan's principal civic activity was the American Legion. Founded in 1919 by veterans returning from World War I, it was later chartered under the *United States Code*. The Legion organized commemorative events and veteran support activities and was also active in national politics, both on behalf of the interests of veterans and on more general political issues. At the state level it was organized into departments. The basic units within each department were the so-called posts that usually represented a single town, city, or part of a county. In the period from World War I extending into the aftermath of the Second World War, the American Legion was a major political force in the United States at the local, state, and national levels.

Luckily for Sullivan, his brief stint in the Navy qualified him to be a member of the Legion, and he enthusiastically jumped into the activities of the Henry J. Sweeney Post No. 2 in Manchester. The Sweeney Post would become perhaps the most important affiliation of his life, in that it provided him a platform of friendships, acquaintances, and name recognition at both the state and national levels that he would call upon throughout his career.

Styles Bridges: Political Campaigns and Beyond

Sullivan's political involvement began in 1928 when he was an active backer of Alfred E. Smith of New York for president. He at first supported Smith again in 1932, gaining some notoriety when he engineered a coup by placing a full slate of Smith-pledged candidates on the ballot for the presidential primary at the last minute. When FDR prevailed, however, Sullivan became a dedicated Roosevelt man forever.

Other than his two successful campaigns to be Hillsborough County solicitor, Sullivan had never run for elected office himself prior to 1934. Nevertheless, as a respected lawyer, by reason of his American Legion activities and his social and civic involvements, he was well-known throughout most of the state. Accordingly, he decided to make a run for governor in that year's election. He captured the Democratic nomination in a tough campaign and faced off against Styles Bridges, the Republican nominee, in the spring, summer, and fall.

Bridges was born and raised in Pembroke, Maine. After graduating from that town's high school, he completed a two-year course at the University of Maine's College of Agriculture and became a gentleman farmer and county agricultural agent. An unhappy marriage ended in divorce, and he moved to New Hampshire and soon became involved in local politics there. He befriended former New Hampshire Governor Robert Perkins Bass and young Norris Cotton. Bridges worked in the 1924 gubernatorial campaign with Cotton, helping John Winant best the other Republican, Frank Knox, who was publisher of the *Manchester Union-Leader*, and then beat Fred Brown, the Democrat. In 1926 Bass chose Bridges as his campaign manager, but they lost out to Old Guard Republican candidates George Moses (Senate) and Huntley Spaulding (governor). After a second marriage, Bridges organized Charles Tobey's successful campaign against Spaulding in 1928, in the process establishing a broad base of friendly support throughout the state. Tobey reciprocated by naming Bridges to be chairman of the Public Service Commission in 1929. When the 1934 campaign for governor arrived, Bridges prevailed over Charles Carroll in the primary and was ready for the challenge from the Democrat, John Sullivan.

Sullivan was a popular party leader and a strong supporter of President Roosevelt and the New Deal, but a vulnerability that surfaced was the French bias against his Irish heritage.

Both candidates directed their substantive arguments at unemployment, labor conditions, and the slumping economy. However, the campaign focused on the personalities of the two men. Sullivan was a glib and articulate speaker who appealed to urban constituents. Bridges was folksy and more appreciated by farmers and rural voters. The race appeared to be close going into the final weekend before the vote on Tuesday, November 6. But on the previous Saturday a rumor spread through Manchester, the state's largest, and strongly Democratic, city. One of the city's issues in the campaign was the demands of the French workers who lived largely on the western side of the Merrimack for a new bridge over that river to facilitate their ability to go to work in the Amoskeag mills. The rumor was that at a private party Sullivan had said, "Let the Frogs jump across." All who knew him instantly saw through the lie, for Sullivan was too sensitive and too shrewd to have made such a statement, but with only a couple of days left before the vote it was too late for Sullivan to effectively counter the rumor. Bridges won by only 2,642 votes, and he got more votes in Manchester's French-speaking ward than any other Republican on the state ticket. Bridges never admitted making the statement, but he also never denied it. The Sullivan camp remained convinced that the canard had cost them the election and that Bridges had effectively stolen it.

Bridges ran successfully for the United States Senate in 1936, prevailing even though FDR carried the state over Alf Landon by four thousand votes.

Always one to find a humorous story in every bad situation no matter how difficult it was to absorb, Sullivan for years laughingly told of one incident that occurred during the campaign: "I came to this small town one day that held only a half-dozen Democrats, the youngest of whom was 72. Well, they were undecided as to whom they would vote for in the primaries. They looked me up and down. I guess I looked pretty young to them. Eventually, I casually mentioned, in outlining my experience, that I had been Mayor of Hanover 15 years previously. That impressed them. 'That being the case, young feller,' snapped the youngest of them, 'I'll see that all of us here vote for you. Mayor of Hanover, you say? Fifteen years ago? That must have been good experience.'"

John L.'s spirits were buoyed on October 20, 1936, when his and Priscilla's first child, a daughter they named Patricia, was born.

Two years later, in 1938, after serving (from 1937 to 1939) as commander of the prestigious New Hampshire Department of the American Legion, Sullivan tried again. John L.'s opponent was the incumbent governor, Francis P. Murphy, a wealthy shoe manufacturer from Nashua who had earlier served in the state legislature. Again it was a tough campaign, but New Hampshire at that point was having doubts about the wisdom of unrequited support for the New Deal that Sullivan strongly supported.

When it was all over, the Republicans held all five of the major political seats in the state—Murphy still in the governorship by 18,413 votes over Sullivan, Bridges and Charles Tobey in the United States Senate, and Foster Stearns and Arthur B. Jenks of Manchester in the U.S. House of Representatives.

The Republicans' victories from 1934 to 1938 marked the beginning of a domination of New Hampshire politics that lasted for over a half century.

Bridges went on to spend twenty-four years in the United States Senate. As a middle-of-the-road Republican he became one of the most powerful men in the Senate. However, his record became tainted in his later years in Washington by allegations that he had accepted large sums of money from various special interest groups.

* * *

John L. carefully edged his new Oldsmobile through the late winter snowfall in March, 1939, down Elm Street toward his office in the Amoskeag Bank building. Not more than a half-dozen mill workers were out at this early hour, slowly trudging their way in the direction of the red-brick factory buildings where spirals of steam were beginning to rise from their tall chimneys. Down the hill to the west a blanket of fog hung over the river. The windshield wiper whacked away at the ice buildup on the glass as Sullivan slowly turned the auto into his parking space in the open lot across from the bank.

Fortunately the heat was still on in the building this Saturday morning, and he soon warmed up in his spacious office, the walls covered with photographs of his important political acquaintances and prestigious clients, some posing with him, some alone. He went right to work attacking the foot-high pile of papers on his desk. Since January he had been wrestling with two serious tax problems for two important clients. He had tried to refer them to a tax counsel in Boston, but both had insisted that he handle the matter himself and told him to bone up on the tax issues involved. He had done that and then written up the details of both cases to the commissioner of Internal Revenue in Washington, Guy Helvering. Not having heard from Helvering, earlier this week Sullivan had called down and made an appointment to see him during the last week of March. The pile of papers on Sullivan's desk mainly related to those two cases, and they needed more intense studying before he left for D.C.

Three hours later, his studying and the unfinished business from the prior day completed, he leaned back in his brown leather chair to rest. As he looked out the window up Elm and over the Merrimack, he was pleased to see that the snow had stopped falling and that the sun was beginning to streak through the gray cloud cover. The snowplows were already out. The St. Patrick's Day parade scheduled for noon would undoubtedly go off on time. He smiled as he thought about leading the parade with his American Legion friends and the party that he and Priscilla were giving that evening at their house in honor of Frank Knox, who was back in town for a board meeting of the newspaper.

As he lit a cigarette, Sullivan's thoughts turned to the course of his life since he had graduated from Harvard Law School and joined his father in this office. He was enjoying his successful law practice, and he was the de facto leader of the Democratic Party in New Hampshire, a man of substantial prestige who was well regarded in both political parties. He loved to tell everyone that, "What a young lawyer in New Hampshire had to do in those days was: run for state representative and lose, run for state senator and lose, run for governor and lose; by then everyone knows you and you've built up a helluva law practice."

But the Depression had taken its toll on New Hampshire and Sullivan's hopes for a significant role there. He yearned for a larger field of battle where he could have a greater impact. Never one to dwell on past failures, he quickly put aside any thoughts about his political defeats. Instead he looked forward, anxious to find another way to move on from New Hampshire and participate at a higher level in the course of the nation's destiny.

Of particular interest and concern to him for many years had been the country's lack of military preparedness, especially as it related to the United States Navy. Ever since the end of World War I, when his own Navy career had been cut short, Sullivan had been closely following developments in the Navy arena with the help of a constant flow of news on the subject from the American Legion.

At the time of the 1922 Washington Naval Treaty, the United States had the second-largest Navy in the world, after Britain. That treaty limited the number of aircraft carriers and battleships that each nation could maintain, and established a 5-5-3 ship ratio among Great Britain, America, and Japan. But thereafter, while other nations were building up naval ships in categories that were not forbidden and increasing the number of airplanes, the United States effectively abandoned all naval construction.

The London Treaty of 1930 extended the ship lists to cruisers, destroyers, and submarines, but by that time the United States was below its permitted ratio in aircraft carriers, and the nation's ships were significantly obsolete in the other areas.

No action was taken by the Congress in the early 1930s to remedy the situation. Finally, in 1933, President Roosevelt set aside $238 million from the Depression general relief fund for the Navy. The following year Congress passed the Vinson-Trammell Act, which authorized (but did not appropriate funds for) new naval construction up to treaty limits and specified that all profits made by shipbuilding companies in excess of 10 percent must be returned to the Treasury.

The Washington and London treaties expired on December 31, 1936, setting off a race in naval shipbuilding throughout the rest of the world. The United States still failed to take action until May 17, 1938, when Congress passed the Naval Expansion Act. Among other things, the act authorized an increase of forty thousand tons in aircraft carriers, thus enabling the beginning of what would become a fleet of *Essex*-class aircraft carriers. Many defense-minded citizens, including John Sullivan, breathed a sigh of relief when that legislation passed.

In 1937 he and Priscilla had spent a month in Europe as part of an American Legion dedication of a number of monuments erected in memory of American soldiers who died during the First World War. During that trip he conferred with a number of European and American officials, including General John J. Pershing. Upon his return, in his report to the Legion's national commander and in press interviews, he expressed the opinion that while the prospects for peace in Europe appeared to have improved with the passing of the Spanish crisis, Europeans remained greatly concerned over the Japan-China undeclared war in China. Unfortunately, his report was transpiring to be overly optimistic.

Sullivan's thoughts on that cold New Hampshire morning were further intensified by recent developments in Europe. Just the day before, the front page of the *Manchester Union-Leader* had reported that Nazi Germany was invading Czechoslovakia. Not surprised in the wake of British Prime Minister Neville Chamberlain's appeasement of Hitler at Munich the previous September, Sullivan nevertheless became more worried. The earlier German aggressions in the Rhineland and Austria combined with the new incursion foreshadowed Hitler's true intentions and a broader war. In his State of the Union message just two months earlier, the president had noted that while the crisis had been temporarily averted, ". . . it has become increasingly clear that world peace is not assured. All about us rage undeclared wars, military and economic. All about us grow more deadly armaments, military and economic. All about us are threats of new aggression, military and economic." Roosevelt's words stirred Sullivan's patriotism.

As he pulled on his heavy overcoat to go out and join the parade, Sullivan began to think that perhaps he should try to find a spot in the country's leadership that would be dealing with these ominous developments. Maybe he should go to Washington and find some significant role in the Roosevelt administration, preferably in the Navy Department. He wondered which, if any, of his many connections might help him secure such a position.

PART II

Washington

3

Connected: Assistant to the U.S.
Commissioner of Internal Revenue

Jim Farley

By dint of his own reputation as a lawyer in Manchester, his political stature in the state as a "deserving Democrat," and his contacts in the American Legion, in September 1939 Sullivan landed in Washington, D.C., as assistant to the commissioner of the Internal Revenue. Years later he described how he got there in a way that downplayed his own ambitions at the time:

> The following week [after meeting with Commissioner Helvering for his two clients] I had a telephone call from Jim Farley asking me if I didn't want to become Assistant Commissioner of Internal Revenue, and I told him that I had no desire for any position with the Federal Government. He said that I had made an impression on Guy Helvering, the Commissioner, and I said that, well, we had just had a knockdown, dragout fight, and Jim said, "Well, I guess he likes the way you fought because he wants you to put on his colors and fight from his corner."

It is significant that it was Jim Farley who first contacted Sullivan about coming down to Washington. James A. Farley had the reputation as a "kingmaker" who had been a key player in Franklin D. Roosevelt's rise to power. He ran FDR's successful New York gubernatorial campaign in 1928 and his presidential campaigns in 1932 and 1936. It is generally acknowledged that he put together the coalition of labor unions, farmers, blacks, and Catholics that powered the New Deal. After the 1932 election he devised and administered the patronage system for the new administration and became chairman of the Democratic National Committee and postmaster general. (In this era the postmaster general was traditionally assigned the political heavy lifting in presidential administrations.) It is believed that Farley first met Sullivan in the early 1930s at an American Legion function. On the eve of the 1936 presidential election Sullivan kept Farley apprised of voting results in New Hampshire.

When Farley called, Sullivan at first played hard to get, masking his enthusiasm:

> I told him I wasn't interested, but I'd drop in and thank Mr. Helvering the next time I was in Washington. And Jim said, "Well, then, will you come to call on me afterwards," which I did. And they both very strongly urged me to take the position. I was unable to accept the position at that time because these two tax cases were pending, and it was not until the following September when the cases were settled that I came to Washington and was sworn in on the 3rd of September, 1939.

About twenty minutes after Sullivan was sworn in, England and France declared war on Germany. He recalled that "right off the bat I was in the middle of things, handling things, which I probably wouldn't have been allowed to touch until I had at least five years' experience."

So John L. had managed to obtain a position that was important. It wasn't a job in the Navy Department, his first choice, but maybe that could come later. At least he was in the high-level decision-making mix, with an opportunity to deal with the Navy from Treasury (the largest portion of his time in the bureau was spent dealing with tax issues as they related to Navy contracts) and with Capitol Hill, where he could bring his political acumen to bear.

4

Assistant Secretary of the Treasury

On January 17, 1940, just over three months after stepping into the Internal Revenue post (after being confirmed by the Senate on January 11), Sullivan was leapfrogged up in the Treasury Department by President Roosevelt to be assistant secretary, a position in which he assumed a major portion of the responsibilities of John Hanes, who was retiring as undersecretary—specifically, all the tax legislation, procurement, the Internal Revenue, and several other bureaus. Sullivan's diary provides some clues as to how he accomplished this leap.

Even before being sworn in, he attended meetings at Treasury on January 2, 4, 5, 8, and 9, attended a White House reception on January 18, and met with Tommy ("the Cork") Corcoran and Claude Pepper, both of whom were in the political upper circle with FDR. On February 6 he recorded his advice to the president on how to approach the upcoming primary in New Hampshire, FDR's view of Jim Farley's apparent intention to throw his hat in the ring along with others to succeed Roosevelt, and the president's concerns about the Navy:

> Prisc[illa] at lunch at White House. Had lunch with Alvie Lucier. Paged and asked to be at White House myself at 1:50. Entered President's office at 2:00. He and Sec[retary of the Treasury Morgenthau] had lunched on his desk. [I] told [the president that an] unpledged delegation [in New Hampshire]

for "him and his policies" would not be feasible. I said I wanted delegation pledged to F.D.R.—said I did *not* want his approval, that if I left the room without his *disapproval* I was satisfied. He seemed to appreciate the technique. He [FDR] then related interview with Farley. "At the end of a conference, out of the blue and apropos of nothing we had discussed before, Jim said 'Have you any objection to my filing in N H.?' What could I say? I finally said 'No.'" He then discussed candidates. "Hull—extremely able, but so old. He'd never get thru a campaign. Farley couldn't be elected President. If he ran for Vice President people would think it a smart trick to bring in the Pope through the back door. The last time I saw my great and good friend Cardinal Mundelein, he warned me against letting a Catholic run for Vice Pres. He said 'We'll have to wait until we get an able Catholic from the open spaces—like Tom Walsh—and run him for the top job.' Garner?" (dismissed with the wave of a hand). We then discussed recent difficulties with the Navy. He expressed complete approval of my action and attitude. Talked of his troubles when he was Ast Sec of Navy: shellac, potato peelers, bandages. We left at about 3. Sec said he had never seen the President so relaxed. . . .

What a day. Ruling in Atlas case ready at 4:15. Sec finally decided I should have a press conference *at once*. Zowie. What a conference.

How I hated to leave for Manchester tonight. Priscilla will [leave] for NY tomorrow so this was our last night in Washington as just a threesome [John L., Priscilla, and daughter Patricia]. And what fun we have had. God has been good.

For Sullivan to be promoted so quickly and to be engaged directly with the president in a significant political discussion was extraordinary. There appear to be two possible explanations of why these events were occurring. As to the quick promotion, it may well have been that Sullivan was targeted for a higher post from the beginning and that the Internal Revenue job was in effect just a "parking spot" until the administration found a better place to utilize his political skills. It was also probable that after Sullivan arrived he did such a good job and impressed his superiors and the White House with his political judgment, that the president felt that his original judgment was confirmed and decided to move John L. up. The historian Paolo Coletta stated that the latter probability was the real reason: "When he [Sullivan] went to Washington in 1939 as an assistant to the Commissioner of Internal Revenue, he appealed so strongly to President Franklin D. Roosevelt that Roosevelt moved him to the Treasury Department as Assistant Secretary."

One clear outgrowth of these developments that quickly became apparent was that Sullivan's role in the Roosevelt administration was to be as much political as technical. At least one of his initial beats was to be Capitol Hill.

Henry Morgenthau, Jr.

Sullivan's boss at the Treasury Department, Secretary Henry Morgenthau, Jr., was an experienced administrator who was one of the principal figures credited with reviving the United States economy after the Great Depression. He had a reputation for selecting first-class assistants and using them effectively. Born in New York City in 1891 into a prosperous German-Jewish family, Morgenthau attended Phillips Exeter Academy and Cornell University, where he received a degree in agriculture. After college his father bought him a large farm of twenty-four hundred acres in Dutchess County, New York, that he named Fishkill Farms, populated by rows of McIntosh apple trees and rose bushes. It was there that he met Franklin Roosevelt in 1915. After World War I he became active in Democratic Party politics, focusing on agricultural issues, rural electrification, and rural education. He worked to get Roosevelt elected governor of New York in 1928 and participated in FDR's 1932 presidential campaign. Brought to Washington by Roosevelt, he began as head of the Farm Credit Administration and then was made secretary of the Treasury in 1934, where he served until just after Roosevelt died. By nature a fiscal conservative, Morgenthau nevertheless went along with FDR's New Deal programs, and in World War II he administered the most rapid expansion of federal expenditures in the country's history. He was one of the first to see the danger posed by Hitler's Germany, and supported aid to the British and French even prior to America's entry into the war. The pinnacle of Morgenthau's career was the Bretton Woods Agreement of 1944 that established a system of fixed rates of currency exchange, the International Monetary Fund, and the World Bank. Morgenthau's nadir occurred when the postwar planning debate began: Morgenthau put forth a vengeful plan that called for the deindustrialization as well as the disarmament of Germany. Secretary of War Henry L. Stimson opposed the Morgenthau Plan, and when the new president, Harry Truman, rejected it, Morgenthau angrily resigned on July 22, 1945. He devoted the rest of his life to assisting Jewish philanthropies. He was a prominent Zionist, serving as chairman of the American Financial and Development Corporation for Israel and as chairman of the Hebrew University in Jerusalem.

During his tenure Morgenthau demonstrated that, while he was very creative in the development of the administration's policies, the implementation phase—the political process of "selling" the programs to a skeptical Congress—was not his strong suit. In this respect, the national press, led by Walter Lippmann of *The New York Herald Tribune*, excoriated Morgenthau for what it perceived to be a poor performance. The secretary also had difficulties dealing with other departments and agencies in the executive branch, including the Navy, War, and State departments.

John Sullivan helped fill these voids in Morgenthau's persona. Although Morgenthau told John L. when he arrived that one of his principal roles would be to deal with the Navy and the Army, Sullivan's main mission initially became acting as Morgenthau's man on the Hill. During Sullivan's tenure as assistant secretary, Treasury sent five major tax bills up to Capitol Hill, and all of them were passed. Sullivan played a key role in the success of the first two of these and an advisory role in the last three. Walter Lippmann later said, "[H]e went to Washington as Assistant Secretary of the Treasury, in which office he strove to repair strained relations between the Treasury and Congress and was brilliant in appearances before congressional committees." During the entire time Sullivan and Morgenthau remained cordial, but wary of each other. It may well have been that Morgenthau was suspicious of Sullivan's relationship with Roosevelt and perhaps also a bit envious of his easy, successful efforts on the Hill. Sullivan for his part recognized and appreciated Morgenthau's great contributions and his loyalty to FDR. He said years later that "they were very, very close. I don't think I ever saw greater loyalty than Morgenthau displayed toward FDR." Sullivan's own relationship with Morgenthau was reported to be strained. If that was true, John L. apparently endeavored to minimize and cover up any difficulties in that regard, for there is no specific remaining evidence of it. After Sullivan completed his term, a *Washington Post* commentator wrote that "In the latter job [Assistant Secretary] Sullivan's principal task was building up the Treasury's Capitol Hill fences, wrecked by Secretary Morgenthau's unfortunate efforts to present tax bills personally to Congress. He was tremendously successful at this." The article added:

> John L. became very popular personally with the newspapermen on the "Treasury run." For he is a very friendly fellow and a real gentleman. One of his chief assets in politics is his "gift for friendship" and his ability to remember the first names of thousands of people. Many Democrats consider him second only to Jim Farley in this regard. [H]e wins his points by logic, quick wit and charm. Above medium height, Sullivan has a pleasant, tanned Irish face with a pointed, upturned nose and curly, brownish-auburn hair. He is a natty dresser.
>
> In politics Sullivan might be described as a middle-roader. He was a great admirer of Franklin D. Roosevelt, yet he has not been an intimate of the extreme leftist New Dealers.

By contrast Henry Morgenthau maintained a stern demeanor, frequently putting off gainsayers rather than persuading them. Arthur Schlesinger, Jr., alluded to this aspect of Morgenthau's personality: "[H]e tended toward worry and suspicion, displaying in official relations a pervading mixture of insecurity and aggressiveness."

An example of how Morgenthau would use Sullivan to handle ticklish situations occurred during Sullivan's first days on the job in January 1940. It was reported that Assistant Secretary of War Louis Johnson had criticized Morgenthau regarding airplane contracts. Morgenthau asked Sullivan to brace Johnson on the matter. Sullivan did so, and Johnson denied the report, but John L. diplomatically but clearly conveyed his secretary's upset. The confrontation forecast what would become Sullivan's style in Washington—toughness, but never to the ad hominem level that would sever an important relationship. Years later this early clash with Johnson would be remembered as both prophetic and ironic.

Almost immediately upon assuming his new position, Sullivan was confronted with efforts by the Navy and War departments to repeal or emasculate the 1934 legislation known as the Vinson-Trammell Act. That act provided a blueprint for a systematic program of ship replacements for the Navy, but only half were actually ever built. It further specified that all profits made by shipbuilders and other military contractors in excess of 10 percent of the contract price should be returned to the Treasury. Both the Navy and the War departments viewed Vinson-Trammell as a deterrent to their efforts to build their military equipment capabilities.

Sullivan was also in constant dialogue with the Army and Navy departments regarding the tax aspects of contracts for the purchases of steel, gunpowder, ammunition, and other military supplies and equipment for companies including the Atlas, Hercules Engine, Curtiss-Wright, United Aircraft, Lukens Steel, DuPont, Pratt and Whitney, Chrysler Corporation, Colt Firearms, and United States Steel. He devised a form of "closing agreement" that cleared U.S. companies to provide needed munitions to Britain and France up to and during the Second World War.

He began a long, tense relationship with Colin Stam, the chief of staff of the Congressional Joint Committee on Internal Revenue Taxation. During their first luncheon meeting, Stam firmly made it clear that the committee and Congress were anxious to avoid any tax legislation in 1940. Sullivan realized immediately that, given Stam's conservatism and feelings of self-importance, he (Sullivan) would have to establish direct relationships with the significant Senate and House leaders themselves in order to accomplish the Treasury Department's objectives in Congress. He began to do just that right away, soon gaining the trust and confidence of Senator Pat Harrison (D-MS), who was chairman of the Senate Finance Committee; Congressman Robert Doughton (D-NC), chairman of the House Ways and Means Committee, who hated deficit spending and believed in "pay-as-you-go"; Speaker of the House Sam Rayburn (D-TX); Senator Arthur Vandenberg (R-MI); Congressman Carl Vinson (D-GA), chairman of the House Naval Affairs Committee, who became known as the father of the two-ocean Navy; Congressman Jere Cooper (D-TN), chairman of a key House subcommittee; Senate Majority Leader Alben Barkley (D-KY), later vice president of the United States under President Harry S. Truman; Senator Walter George (D-GA); Senator Harry Byrd (D-VA); and Senator William King (D-UT).

John L. was full of joy in late February when son Charles was born on the 25th.

Sullivan spent a great deal of time from February to May 1940 negotiating a revision of the Vinson-Trammell Act with these principals on Capitol Hill, particularly Harrison, Vinson, Doughton, and Cooper, that would enable contractual and tax amortization of losses over four years, and defeating corporate and Navy Department pressure on Congress to permit full profit deficiencies to be spread over the same extended periods. The Navy's original proposal, arguably based on the Navy's concern about contractors not bidding for ships, would have, in Sullivan's view, vitiated the central purpose of Vinson-Trammell, which was to prohibit excess profits. Notwithstanding his admiration for the Navy, he thereby established early on that he was not going to be its lapdog on tax issues. On a separate matter, he supported a reasonable Navy request for a $6 million appropriation for expansion of armor plate facilities.

As the likelihood of American involvement in the war in Europe grew, he also found himself resolving such legal issues as the appropriate tax treatment of property abandoned by munitions makers at the end of the war. His daily advice to Morgenthau regarding the political implications of Treasury Department decisions grew in importance during the same period. During the March primary in New Hampshire for the upcoming fall presidential election, Sullivan became the designated Treasury spokesman, fending off questions from the likes of Drew Pearson and other newspaper and radio reporters. Similarly, he fielded all press questions relating to a tax investigation of Paul McNutt, the former Democratic governor of Indiana who had initially refused to support Roosevelt's run for president. Sullivan strongly asserted that politics was playing no part in the investigation.

In the middle of May, fiscal pressures on the Treasury Department increased significantly, and activity escalated. In a May 17 meeting Senator Harrison and Congressman Cooper reiterated to Sullivan that they hoped it would be possible to postpone both any tax program and any bill to raise the debt limit until 1941. On the same day, Assistant Secretary of War Louis Johnson sent a memorandum to President Roosevelt forwarding and recommending legislation to permit military procurement without competition at the direction of the president. Sullivan quickly composed an opposing Treasury memo stating that such legislation was ill-advised based on earlier experience in both the United States and the U.K. during the World War of 1914 to 1918.

These developments were examples among many reflecting events in the outside world impacting Treasury. The month of May transpired to be the culmination of a year-and-a-half deterioration of the situation in Europe since British Prime Minister Chamberlain's Munich agreement postulating "peace in our time."

Facing strong isolationist sentiment in an election year, Roosevelt at first felt effectively hamstrung. In his January 1939 State of the Union speech he requested Congress to provide an additional $525 million for defense, $450 million for the Army (of which two-thirds was to purchase airplanes, there being no separate Air Force at the time), $65 million for the Navy, and $10 million to train civilian air pilots. The request languished in the conservative Congress, partly because Roosevelt continued to shy away from declaring outright that war was inevitable.

Then, on August 23, 1939, Hitler shocked the world by signing a nonaggression pact with the Soviet Union. Days later, pursuant to a secret understanding between the two countries,

German troops stormed across Poland. Britain and France declared war on Germany and Chamberlain brought Winston Churchill back into the British government. Roosevelt now moved quickly, asking Congress to repeal the embargo provisions of the 1937 Neutrality Act that prohibited the sale of arms to nations at war or to carry arms in U.S. ships for other belligerents. Congress balked in an early vote but finally passed the measure on November 2. The way was thereby cleared for FDR to supply aid to Britain and France. The president also now had the support of a strong new Army chief of staff—General George C. Marshall.

On April 9, 1940, Hitler struck again: German troops occupied both Denmark and Norway. Chamberlain's credibility was completely shot; he resigned on May 10 and was succeeded by Winston Churchill. On the same day, Germany moved into Belgium and Holland. Churchill cabled Roosevelt pleading for help before it was too late.

Roosevelt asked a joint session of Congress for a supplemental defense appropriation of $1.2 billion and then asked for an additional $1.9 billion. One year later Congress had responded by appropriating $37.3 billion for defense, four times the entire 1939 federal budget. Airplanes, antiaircraft weapons, and steel immediately began to flow to England, but Churchill's request for destroyers was withheld because it required a special Congressional authorization.

The situation in France continued to worsen. German troops surrounded the French First Army, a British Expeditionary Force of nearly 350,000, and the Belgian Army against the North Sea at the town of Dunkirk. The Belgians surrendered, but 338,226 British and French soldiers escaped across the Channel in a massive sealift between May 27 and June 4. All their equipment and ammunition was left behind. Britain had saved its Army, but it was bereft of the means to fight.

Roosevelt let it be known that he wanted to help the British in every way possible. General Marshall rose to the occasion, designating what was needed as surplus and arranging with the Treasury Department, in the persons of John L. Sullivan and General Counsel Edward Foley, for the equipment to be sold to Curtiss-Wright and U.S. Steel, and those companies then resold it to Britain at cost. FDR's biographer Jean Edward Smith concluded, "Except for tanks, which were in short supply, the British Army was substantially rearmed within six weeks after returning from Dunkirk."

On June 10, 1940, another hammer fell. Italy declared war on France and launched its divisions through the Alpine passes. Roosevelt was livid. In a speech later that evening to the graduating class at the University of Virginia School of Law in Charlottesville he scorned, "On this tenth day of June, 1940, the hand that held the dagger has struck it into the back of its neighbor." He also quietly decided that it was time to beef up his fighting team. In the next few days he relieved both Secretary of the Navy Charles Edison and Secretary of War Harry Woodring of their duties.

On June 19, just before the Republican convention, Roosevelt announced that Colonel Frank Knox, the progressive publisher of the *Chicago Daily News*, would replace Edison at the Navy Department and that Henry L. Stimson, a widely respected New York lawyer who had been Hoover's secretary of state and Taft's secretary of war, would become his own secretary of war. Both men were Republicans. In a masterful political stroke the president thereby gained two powerful conservatives on his team, isolating the isolationists.

Frank Knox

Frank Knox was one of Manchester, New Hampshire's, most significant citizens in the first half of the twentieth century. Born in Boston in 1874, he moved to Michigan with his parents and graduated from Alma College there. He then served in Cuba with Teddy Roosevelt's Rough Riders. Upon returning to Michigan he became a newspaper reporter in Grand Rapids and before long garnered ownership of the *Sault Ste Marie Evening News*. He also became involved in politics and from 1910 to 1912 he was chairman of Michigan's Republican State Central Committee, but his progressive views soon alienated the state's old guard.

In 1912 he sold his paper and moved to New England where he established, with partner John Muehling, a new progressive newspaper in Manchester that he named the *Leader*. In 1913 he bought out the competing *Union*, and the paper became the *Manchester Union-Leader*. He supported Theodore Roosevelt's

Progressive ticket in 1912. When the United States entered World War I, he joined the First New Hampshire Infantry Regiment, and by the end of the war he was a major in the artillery. After the war he was elected the first state commander of the New Hampshire American Legion. In 1923 he ran for governor of New Hampshire, but he was defeated in the Republican primary by John Winant.

Early on during his time in Manchester, Knox became a close personal friend and client of both Patrick Sullivan and his son, John.

In 1927 William Randolph Hearst hired Knox to run the three Hearst newspapers in Boston and in 1928 made him general manager of all twenty-seven of his national dailies.

In 1931 Knox capped his newspaper career when he took control of the *Chicago Daily News*, which he managed until 1940.

In 1936, after a successful fund-raising effort for the Republican Party in 1934, he became the Republican candidate for vice president in Alf Landon's unsuccessful run against FDR. Although he had vociferously attacked Roosevelt's domestic agenda, Knox remained a strong supporter of the president's foreign policies, and in 1940 FDR appointed Knox to be secretary of the Navy, a post that he held until 1944. As secretary, Knox was responsible for building up the Navy to fight both the Germans and the Japanese.

Knox continued to own the *Manchester Union-Leader* until his death in 1944, when the paper was purchased by William Loeb, who veered the paper's editorial policy sharply to the right. Even though Knox's work took him away from New Hampshire from 1927 on, he retained his residence in the northwest section of Manchester, principally as a vacation home, and remained close to the Sullivans. John Sullivan and Knox were and would always remain mutual supporters.

Preparing for War: Financing the Huge Cost

The events of May 1940 in Europe hit the Treasury like a flash of lightning. When Sullivan had moved into the assistant secretary slot in January, the feeling throughout Washington, notwithstanding the protests of the isolationists, was that it was inevitable that the United States would soon become involved in the war in Europe. But Dunkirk brought the real situation home with a thunderclap.

Those inside the Treasury Department suddenly realized the enormity of the task that was now theirs—raising the vast sums of money that it was going to take to pay for that coming war.

Their options were limited. The United States Government could finance the cost of war in only four ways: higher taxes; reductions in other, nonwar, spending; borrowing from the public; and money creation (for example, in World War II via the Federal Reserve's purchase of government bonds; in effect, the Fed made a loan to the government of newly printed money). Taxation, the usual first resort, was expected to be the way they would raise most of what was needed; but when they looked at the numbers Morgenthau and his team became fearful. The sum was so large that they were genuinely concerned about a taxpayer revolt. Ultimately they spread the cost as widely as they could, utilizing all four methods.

John Sullivan played a major role in the two most important of these efforts: first, in shepherding Treasury's initial increased tax bills through the Congress, and then in the selling of U.S. war bonds. In his first weeks on the job, Sullivan jumped right into these issues that would consume him throughout the next four years.

Treasury's preliminary calculations in January 1940 were that the country was facing an estimated budget deficit of $2.9 billion for the fiscal year ending June 30, 1941, and the estimate for national defense expenditures was $1.9 billion. A revised estimate in the spring put the defense number at $3.2 billion, which was the number the president requested in a message to Congress on May 11. His message was soon followed by a measure for national conscription that would require substantial additional funds. Treasury was also concerned about the strictures of the $45 billion debt limit, of which only a working balance of just over $1 billion remained.

*   *   *

At six o'clock in the morning of Monday, May 27, 1940, John Sullivan was already at his desk in the Treasury Building, reviewing draft legislation prepared by staff over the weekend. A shaft of bright sunlight shone through a window and across his desk as he sipped black coffee, carefully studying each word and sentence and making notes in the margins of the pages.

By eight-thirty a.m. he had completed his review and refined his comments. He packed his file folder and hurried down the hall to Morgenthau's office where he joined the secretary, Senator Harrison, and Congressman Cooper, as well as Dan Bell and Guy Helvering from the department. Also present as an outside adviser was Roswell Magill, a New York lawyer who was a partner in the prestigious firm of Cravath, Swaine and Moore, and who had served as assistant secretary of the Treasury in 1937 and 1938.

Senator Harrison and Congressman Cooper immediately opened the discussion by objecting to any tax bill at this time, noting that both the president and Congress hoped that Congress would adjourn before June 15 so the political parties could prepare for their national conventions in June and July. Harrison thought it would be preferable to increase the national debt. Neither liked an excess profits tax, preferring straight across-the-board tax rate increases on corporations. Senator Harrison stated that in his opinion the country was more seriously confused than it was in the early months of 1917.

Sullivan bided his time as the others offered their comments, mostly favorable, to the secretary. Finally he spoke up, objecting strenuously to several provisions, including those retroactively levying an additional tax on 1939 income. There followed a heated discussion in which Harrison and Cooper gradually came around to the prospect of an increase in both taxes and the debt limit, subject to the effort being labeled as a national defense bill rather than a deficit bill, and they agreed to call meetings of the Democratic members of their respective committees, Senate Finance and House Ways and Means. At the end, Morgenthau directed Sullivan, Helvering, Magill, and Bell to prepare a revised set of tax proposals. They proceeded to a separate conference room and worked through lunch, delivering the new proposals at two-thirty that afternoon. The group had agreed to eliminate the tax on 1939 income, but unanimously recommended that the passage of the new bill should be accompanied by an act raising the debt limit by $5 billion. Morgenthau said he would go over the proposals in the morning with Senator Harrison and Congressman Doughton, chairman of Ways and Means.

At three-twenty Tom Stokes of Scripps Howard telephoned Sullivan regarding a new Navy bill that would transfer supervision of Vinson-Trammell from Treasury to the Navy. Sullivan told him that Treasury strongly opposed the bill.

On Tuesday morning, the 28th, the tax group reconvened in Morgenthau's office at nine o'clock, joined by Colin Stam from the Joint Committee on Taxation. The secretary reported that he had talked with the president, who had suggested that there be a 10 percent tax increase on everything except customs fees on goods from those countries with which the United States had trade agreements. Harrison and Cooper gave reports on their polls of the Democratic members of their committees, which revealed mixed feelings. There followed a discussion of a suggestion by Senator Harrison for a manufacturers' sales tax, which was ultimately rejected.

The group next proceeded to draw up a list of specific tax increases that, in addition to a 10 percent super tax on personal and corporate income taxes, included levies on liquor and gasoline. When the discussion was completed, the secretary telephoned the president and got his approval, whereupon the conferees drafted a statement to issue to the press. It was understood by all that they could expect strong opposition to the proposals from the Republican side of the aisle.

At five-thirty p.m. on the same day Sullivan met in Congressman Doughton's office with Doughton, Congressman Cooper, and Senator Harrison. When asked about Treasury's progress on the tax bill, Sullivan astounded them all by replying that he would have a bill mimeographed and in their hands by nine o'clock the following morning. The group from Capitol Hill then appeared to change their positions completely and to be in favor of speedy action. During the rest of the afternoon and into that evening, Sullivan led a group from Treasury, Stam, and Middleton Beaman, House legislative counsel, in a crash bill-writing session that lasted until eleven-thirty p.m. when the mimeograph team took over.

Sullivan headed to the Hill with multiple copies of the bill the next morning for a ten o'clock meeting of the full Ways and Means Committee, where the Republican members began a series of objections, including a demand for public hearings. Afterward Sullivan went to Senator Harrison's office, who reported that the Senate Republicans were resisting any form of tax bill or debt limit increase. Sullivan attended an informal meeting of the Senate Finance Committee with both Democrats and Republicans in attendance. In addition to the Republican objections, he heard Senator Robert La Follette, the Wisconsin Progressive, call for a thorough revision of the tax code now, not next year, also claiming that expenditure reduction should precede tax increases.

On May 31 both Sullivan and Morgenthau testified before the House Ways and Means Committee in support of the new tax bill.

The Congress acted with unusual swiftness. The House passed the bill on June 11. It was reported to the full Senate with a number of amendments on June 15 and promptly passed. The differences between the House and Senate bills were quickly worked out in conference, and the president signed the legislation on June 25.

The final bill increased tax revenues by over $1 billion a year. It reduced personal exemptions, increased individual and corporate taxes by about 10 percent, increased middle-class surtax rates, and increased excise taxes. At the same time the national debt limit was raised by $4 billion. As large as it was, the new legislation was in reality just a quick stopgap, psychologically preparing the American public for the much greater economic and human sacrifices that were soon to come.

Within days after the president signed the first revenue bill of 1940, Sullivan was back with his team at Treasury, hard at work on a second, more difficult piece of tax legislation. By July 8 they were ready to discuss it with President Roosevelt. After a breakfast at the Washington Hotel with Roswell Magill and Randolph Paul, a second New York tax lawyer who was then also an outside adviser but who would later go inside at Treasury, Sullivan met at the White House with Morgenthau, the two New York lawyers, and Ed Foley, Treasury's general counsel, to present their proposals to the president.

The thrust of the proposals was to prevent war profiteering. The vehicle was to be an excess profits tax that would apply just to corporations, not to individuals. The president asked about the applicability to personal trusts, recalling a bitterness that had flowed from a 1937 presentation by Senator Morgenthau to the House Ways and Means Committee; he was assured that such trusts would be covered. It was also explained to him that a corporate profit between 4 and 10 percent of invested capital was considered to be "standard" and hence exempt from such a tax.

The president gave his preliminary approval to Treasury's general approach, but he said that he did not want to be permanently committed to specific proposals and wanted at least twenty-four hours to think the matter through before he took it to the Congress.

Later that evening, Paul and Foley dined at Sullivan's home. After dinner they were joined by a group from the National Defense Council to discuss the impact of the excess profits tax proposal on the Navy and War departments. That group supported the proposal, but they were concerned that both departments would quickly need new facilities that should be given rapid amortization to facilitate and expedite their building. The group also felt that Vinson-Trammell should be repealed because that law was essentially an excess profits tax as well, thereby discriminating against defense contractors if both taxes were to apply to them. Sullivan acknowledged the point, but he felt Vinson-Trammell should just be suspended, not repealed altogether, and he stated that if the amortization provisions were too liberal, the purposes of checking exorbitant wartime profits and raising substantial revenue would be subverted.

Following drafting meetings on the 9th, Sullivan and Morgenthau met with the president and Steve Early, Roosevelt's press secretary, along with Senator Harrison and Congressman Cooper, for the purpose of finalizing a press release announcing the introduction of the new excess profits tax legislation. It concluded that, "The conferees were agreed that the plan is certain to result in an appreciable acceleration of the national defense program. At the same time it is intended that there be no substantial sacrifice of revenues accruing to the United States Treasury." Sullivan agreed to have the bill prepared by July 22.

A pertinent interlude occurred on July 19 when Sullivan spent the afternoon and evening with Frank Knox, his old friend and the new secretary of the Navy, on board the Navy yacht *Sequoia*. Knox also had Colonel "Wild Bill" Donovan aboard. Donovan had been a classmate of FDR's at Columbia Law School and, although Donovan was a Republican, Roosevelt had come to trust the judgment of the World War I Medal of Honor recipient, who would soon head up the Office of Strategic Services in the European theater, and had seen to it that Donovan was used for important, discrete assignments. Sullivan's report to Morgenthau on what transpired on the *Sequoia* is intriguing:

> Secretary Knox explained to me that Colonel Donovan was flying to England the next afternoon and asked me to talk confidentially with him.
>
> Colonel Donovan and I withdrew to another part of the boat and Donovan explained to me that he was going to England on a private mission for Secretary Knox to find out certain things and asked me to write out a set of questions regarding that phase of English tax policy about which I would like certain information. Accordingly I gave him a list of the following questions:

> 1. To what extent is current revenue financing current expenditures?
> 2. What proportion of current revenue is borne by consumers' taxes?
> 3. Is John Q. Public now ready to pay thru the nose?
> 4. How does the man on the street feel about capital levies? And the man who has capital to be levied upon?
> 5. Is the Treasury satisfied with its excess profits plan? Is industry? Is the public?

In the following days Sullivan's close relationship with Knox worked to facilitate interagency relations. John L.'s diary notes that he and Knox discussed taxation and defense issues on a number of occasions, including the amortization of armor plate manufacturing by Bethlehem Steel and Carnegie-Illinois Steel Company.

On July 23 Sullivan and Morgenthau met again with the president to update him on the progress of the bill and related issues. They first showed Roosevelt the present and prospective deficit figures: "the President was agreeably surprised that the figures were not higher." But then, when informed of the Defense Council's desire to separate the amortization provisions from the excess profits tax bill, the president was upset and instructed Sullivan to inform the council "that he was on record, that he had assured the American public there would be no amortization and no repeal of the Vinson-Trammell Act until there was an excess profits tax." Later that day Sullivan relayed this directive to the council, which immediately backed off.

The next week, on Monday July 29, Colin Stam of the Joint Committee shocked the administration by presenting an alternative plan as a substitute for the Treasury's excess profits tax bill. This step precipitated a legislative firestorm that would last for over two months before it was resolved.

The principal difference in Stam's plan was that he proposed using average income received during the four-year period (1936 to 1939) in place of Treasury's definition of excess profits as those in excess of a normal percentage of invested capital as the basis for computing excess profits. Sullivan fired back at the Stam plan the next day:

1. It penalizes defense industries.
2. It forces poor corporations to bear a large part of the burden.
3. It encourages monopoly.
4. It stifles future development of new or small corporations.
5. It gives no consideration to changing capital structure.
6. It is incapable of expansion to yield large revenue. If it carries a tax rate of 100% it could not yield more than $750 millions.

7. It completely disregards the principle of taxing
with regard to ability to pay.

On July 30 Sullivan and Stam faced off before the Senate and House committee members, who appeared quite confused and of many different views as to where to go next. Afterward, on August 2, Chairman Doughton informed Sullivan that "unless we agreed with Stam's plan we would not have a bill in less than three or four months." Sullivan nevertheless stuck to his position.

Sullivan and Morgenthau agreed that they would have to communicate with the president about the situation. Sullivan advised the secretary that even "the combining of the Treasury plan and the Stam plan created a monstrosity which would probably become the worst piece of tax legislation that had ever been on the books." Ever politically astute, however, Sullivan knew the president wanted and needed a bill of some sort and needed it quickly. In order to adhere to the immediate objective of having the House Ways and Means Subcommittee report out some sort of bill no matter how flawed, he drafted a letter from Morgenthau to the president indicating that Treasury would not sponsor or approve the committee bill but would "accept" it by offering no objection. Sullivan correctly foresaw that the administration could be embarrassed by the Stam plan if it were to be embraced.

Unexpectedly, it was Senator La Follette who afforded Sullivan a substantive way out of the dilemma. La Follette sent word to Sullivan that he wanted to see him. They met in the corridor of the Senate office building following Sullivan's testimony to House Ways and Means. Sullivan recorded that:

> Senator La Follette seemed to understand the situation completely. He remarked that we had made an effort to write a real excess profits tax bill and he asked if I would get in touch with him some evening so that he and I could get together without anyone knowing about [it]. He was apparently anxious to help and I believe he will very readily sponsor the Treasury bill if we wish him to do so.

With La Follette was Senator James Clark, Democrat from Missouri, who stated that he would not vote in favor of a bill like the one proposed by Stam.

That same afternoon, Eliot Janeway of *Time* magazine called Sullivan from New York and told him of La Follette's position, which Sullivan of course already knew but did not acknowledge. Janeway also reported that Senator Charles McNary of Oregon, the Republican Senate minority leader, "was going to fight the bill on the floor as being a sham and a hollow shell and he thought I would like to have the information because it looked as though the play was to take credit for the bill away from the Administration." Possibly the game was changing. Sullivan immediately phoned Morgenthau to inform the secretary of these developments.

On the following Monday, Sullivan reported the information about McNary to Harrison and Doughton, who were both unimpressed, apparently because of the low regard for McNary's ability to achieve his stated objective. Nor was Senator Alben Barkley concerned when the same information was given to him.

Sullivan then suggested to the House committee leaders that he and Stam get together to attempt to work out a compromise. They did so and made some progress, but Sullivan learned on August 23 that Stam had gone back on his agreements. Stam's duplicity in that regard assured him the lasting disrespect of Sullivan, who placed a man's word above all else. On that same day Sullivan recorded:

> I finally learned from Doughton the . . . reason for his objection to the Treasury plan. . . . The American Tobacco Company has gone through a reorganization and has had an opportunity to expand its capital. This he felt would give it a terrific advantage over the R.J. Reynolds Company [his own constituent].

Sullivan tried to explain the flaws in Doughton's understanding, and that the Treasury bill would not affect his constituent, but to no avail. Congressman Cooper, on the other hand, remained staunchly opposed to the House (Stam) bill, claiming it would never pass the full committee.

The next day, the president, learning of the impasse in the subcommittee, spoke with Sullivan and asked him to meet again with Stam and the House Ways and Means people to work out something that would free up the bill. After long conferences the following day, a Sunday, Sullivan achieved a breakthrough by changing the rate schedule from percentage brackets to brackets in terms of dollars and getting Stam to agree that the corporations using the average earnings option would pay a privilege tax graduated from 5 to 10 percent. He also seized upon a major provision from Senator La Follette's proposed amendment exempting small corporations from the excess profits tax, thereby simultaneously solving one of Sullivan's own main concerns.

The Democrats then proceeded to schedule joint hearings before Senate Finance and House Ways and Means. The emerging bill, which gave corporate taxpayers the option of using either the Treasury or the Stam option, was pushed through the House under a stringent gag rule. It was passed on August 29 without a roll call and with no dissenting votes.

Differences in the Senate were more difficult to overcome, and it was three weeks before the bill reached the Senate floor. Sullivan testified at an additional hearing of the Senate Finance Committee on September 4 and worked with that committee on September 6 to insert a number of improvements over the House bill. On the 8th, the president spoke to Morgenthau on the telephone, expressing gratitude for Sullivan's successful collaboration with Senator La Follette. For the first time the president appeared to be up to speed on the details of the legislation and "for the first time in putting over the Treasury bill."

On September 11 both Sullivan and Morgenthau appeared before the Senate Finance Committee in executive session. The Treasury representatives were pummeled from nearly all sides for their aggressive involvement in formulating a Senate bill to the administration's own satisfaction. Appropriate mea culpas were offered and the bill stayed intact. The committee voted out the bill later that month; it passed the full Senate quickly thereafter with forty-six yeas and twenty-two (mostly Republican) nays. After a quick conference ironing out the differences between the House and Senate versions, it was delivered to the president, who signed it into law on October 8, 1940.

It was projected that the act would increase revenues by $500 million in calendar year 1940 and by $900 million per year when the defense program became fully operative. Ultimately the nation's needs to finance the war would become higher, but Sullivan's successful efforts in passing the two Revenue Acts of 1940 had put the country on an economic course that would thereafter be much smoother.

* * *

When Jim Farley called Sullivan in early 1939 about coming to Washington, Farley, in the widely accepted expectation that Roosevelt would not run for an unprecedented third term, was already contemplating a presidential bid of his own. He misread Roosevelt's position on whether he would run again, and later felt betrayed when Roosevelt adopted Sullivan's advice about how to approach the New Hampshire primary on the national level by not expressly and publicly seeking a third term, but by accepting a draft. On March 7 Sullivan recorded Farley's reaction:

> Bill Bray called to ask me to see Farley at 12:30. Went over and rode back to Treasury in [Farley's] car. What an interview. He was cordial but very much agitated. As we left the building he took my arm, turned me around to face him and said, "I want you to know the President told me to do what I started to do in N.H." I told him I had no reason to doubt him. He said, "I wish you had seen me before you went up. The trouble around this town is that too many people pretend to speak for the President. I could have told you what he wanted." We entered his car and he proceeded to unburden himself. "I love my country, and my party. And I'm going to look after Farley too. I'm still National Chairman and I'm organizing the Convention. They've got to come to me and they should realize it. Listen! The President actually gave me the date on which he

was going to announce that he would not run again! What was I to do? I'm trying to stay on the road. I'm not going to get mad because then I'm licked. Whom the gods destroy they first make mad." I asked him if he had discussed with the President recently. He said, "What could I say? You can't call the President of the U.S. a liar and then stay in his cabinet. There's only four months to go until the Convention and I'm going to stick it out." He then reminded me that I had promised to keep this confidential and said that Mrs. Farley, O'Connell, and Ronan were the only others who knew about the date the President intended to renounce.

Lunch with Secretary and Foley. Discussion re Indiana. After lunch Sec called to see if I wished to see him *alone*. Went in, explained I had pledged secrecy, but advised him Farley conversation in no way involved him or Treas. He was content.

. . . Learned that Sec and President last night conferred . . . before interviewing me about taxes! . . . Our only conclusion is that this must be part of a general plan to scuttle Vinson Trammell.

Farley's earlier courting of Sullivan undoubtedly reflected Farley's incipient plan to have a strong supporter in the Granite State, particularly one who was Catholic like himself. The irony is that when Farley resigned both his posts after the 1940 Chicago convention had rejected him and nominated Roosevelt for president again and Henry Wallace to be vice president, FDR would seek advice regarding the Catholic vote not from Farley, but from Sullivan, who was said to be quite like Farley in personality and style.

Whether Roosevelt should be nominated and elected to a third term, breaking the unbroken precedent set by George Washington, was causing great consternation throughout the country and even within the Democratic Party itself. At the Democratic convention starting on July 15, Farley, who controlled who got tickets to the gallery, had appeared at first to be in a strong position to grab the nomination of the delegates, who had had no direction from the president. FDR was not in attendance, staying in Washington out of a fear that if there he would have to make promises he would not want to or could not deliver on. In his stead he sent his popular wife, Eleanor, who was warmly received. Senator Alben Barkley delivered a rousing keynote speech in which he announced at the end that his message from the president was that they were all free to vote for any candidate. After moments of confusion they reacted as FDR had hoped, with chants of "We want Roosevelt! We want Roosevelt!" resounding through Chicago Stadium. Farley and other potential candidates backed away, and FDR was handily nominated for an unprecedented third term. At the president's request, and with Eleanor's floor support, Henry Wallace was nominated to be vice president.

Both before and after the convention, Britain, in the persons of King George VI and Winston Churchill, was pleading with the United States to send destroyers to thwart the damaging effects of Germany's U-boats on the English Navy and shipping. After extensive political soul-searching and legal analysis within the administration, on September 3, 1940, the president announced a Destroyers for Bases Agreement whereby American destroyers were exchanged for leases on British bases in the West Indies and Newfoundland. The United Kingdom paid for the ships in gold under a "cash and carry" procedure as required by the Neutrality Acts of the 1930s. Over the protests of Capitol Hill isolationists, public opinion was strongly supportive of the president's action, which also provided a strong boost to his election campaign. When the votes were finally counted on November 6, FDR prevailed in the electoral college by 449 votes to Republican Wendell Willkie's 82. The Democrats also secured control of both the House and the Senate.

* * *

Within days of the election and hardly two months after passage of the Second Revenue Act of 1940, Sullivan received a telephone call from FDR's aide, General ("Pa") Watson, who said, "John, the President is having a little meeting to discuss taxes . . . he wants you there." The "little meeting," which would lead to a huge legislative battle and a dramatic result, was set for November 29. In preparation for that, Sullivan and his team worked up a suggested tax program, which they presented to Morgenthau on the 26th. In an effort to uncover ways to tap major new sources of revenue, their major proposal was a repeal of the tax exemption for interest on future issues of federal, state, and municipal securities—this to be in the first tax bill and a separate one. Other suggestions were mainly rate increases on many items including income sur-taxes, estate and gift taxes, and excise taxes. They stated that they remained opposed to the imposition of general sales taxation. After Morgenthau's review and at his request, Sullivan's group prepared additional supporting data.

At the White House dinner meeting at seven-thirty in the evening on the 29th, attended by Senators Harrison and George, Congressmen Doughton and Cooper, along with Morgenthau, Sullivan, and Dan Bell from Treasury, and Director of the Budget Harold Smith, the president, having heard in the interim from Morgenthau regarding the country's desperate need for substantial additional revenue, did most of the talking, focusing on the group from Congress and urging them to act quickly and strongly. He also assured everyone that he was going to "cut to the bone" other expenses that were not necessary. He said that he thought the Works Progress Administration could be reduced by half, and gave the example of the thousand WPA workers in the Norfolk Navy Yard, half of whom had been added to the regular Navy payrolls. In response, Doughton and Cooper expressed grave concerns about eliminating the exemption for interest on government securities. Nevertheless, it was agreed by all that a strong effort would be made to pass a major tax bill in 1941. The group also discussed the necessity of raising the debt limit and a revision of Social Security taxes to eliminate the method of the federal government's matching the contribution by the states and to substitute a uniform minimum contribution by the federal government, a step toward the ultimate objective of having the federal government assume full responsibility and administration of Social Security.

Having received the president's blessing to proceed, Sullivan, Morgenthau, Dan Bell, and Ed Foley began a series of meetings with the Hill leadership, starting with Speaker Rayburn, to line up support for the legislation. As in the conference with the president, Morgenthau made it clear to Rayburn that the national debt limit would also have to be increased immediately by at least $500 million.

During the following week, Sullivan went on the road, traveling to meetings with the governors and mayors of the major northeastern states to test the feasibility of repealing the exemption for interest on government securities. The reaction was tepid at best. Some agreed to support the plan. Others only said they would not oppose it or that they would say that it was timely to review the issue.

On January 23, the Treasury team met again with the president, who approved what they were doing, including the immediate issuance of $500 million national defense notes. He went even further, discussing the raising of an additional $1 billion and the refunding of $3.25 billion of maturities in March.

Sullivan was inundated by a variety of issues in February and March. On February 10 he issued a Treasury Department press release announcing that corporations could apply for relief from harsh, unanticipated results of the 1940 Excess Profits Tax Act in abnormal situations. Legislative general relief from that act was also required, which Sullivan worked out with Colin Stam; and then, in order to meet a severe time requirement, he worked a procedural coup in Congress by attaching the provisions to the Public Debt Act and getting the House to pass the combined legislation on the same day that it was passed in the Senate. Congressman Doughton told Sullivan that he believed that it was the only time such expedited action had ever been taken. The elimination of inequities cleared the way for future rate raises to that tax.

On March 4, Attorney General Jackson and Secretary of War Stimson requested introduction of a bill to prevent states and municipalities from levying taxes on contractors doing defense work on a cost-plus-fixed-fee basis. Sullivan advised Morgenthau that such a bill would be the end of their attempt to repeal the exemption for interest on state and local securities. He prepared a letter from Morgenthau to the president objecting to the Jackson-Stimson measure.

During this same period a number of congressmen on Ways and Means and senators on the Finance Committee became upset when various newspaper stories on tax developments indicated that new tax provisions were emanating from Treasury officials rather than the Congress. Sullivan stepped in to quell this turf jealousy on the Hill and simultaneously spoke to and fended off a bevy of aggressive Washington reporters, including the young Bob Kintner, then the *New York Herald Tribune's* White House correspondent who later became head of ABC and NBC and then President Lyndon Johnson's Cabinet secretary.

Sullivan and Morgenthau met alone with President Roosevelt on April 11, 1941, to review the current revision of the tax proposals and their impact on 1942 tax collections. They pointed out to the president that the figures set forth reflected a billion-dollar increase over the numbers he had sent to Congress in the budget. The president approved the $3.5 billion target. He then looked at each of the proposed rate increases and indicated his approval. Sullivan recorded further that:

> After we arose to leave, he said he had talked with a friend of his from Aiken who said he was the only liberal in Aiken. This gentleman advised the President there were between two and three hundred families in Aiken with net incomes of $200,000 and the President asked this gentlemen how those families would get along if the tax law were to take from them everything over $100,000, and this gentleman said they would get along all right. Secretary Morgenthau said that we would go to work upon his idea.

Clearly the president had gotten the message as to the severity of the country's need for more revenue.

During the months of April, May, and June, Sullivan met many times in private and executive sessions with the members of the House Ways and Means Committee in an effort to resolve differences over the provisions of the 1941 tax bill. In the course of these discussions it became apparent that there was a deep philosophical divide between Sullivan and Stam. Sullivan's continuing approach was to protect small business and relatively poor individuals; Stam's point of view was essentially Republican—not to overburden the wealthy and their big corporations. Thus from their very first meeting on April 16, Stam wanted to lower the revenue target from $3.5 to $2 billion because he feared that the higher burden would upset business. He also opposed raising estate tax rates and pushed for a payroll tax against all workers. After a while Treasury conducted some conferences directly with senators and congressmen, both Democrat and Republican, but without Stam present, to take place in the evenings at Morgenthau or Sullivan's homes in attempts to break logjams on specific issues.

On April 24, Sullivan testified before the Ways and Means Committee in open session, summarizing the Treasury's positions on the tax program to that point. He outlined the governing principles of the administration's approach:

> . . . [F]irst, that the greater part of the cost of the emergency defense program should be met from current taxes rather than borrowing; second, that these taxes should be collected with a minimum of interference with the effective mobilization of all our manpower, managerial capacity, business enterprise, and national resources; and, third, that the additional tax burden necessitated by the emergency should be distributed equitably among the several segments of our population.

He added specifically that current taxes should provide approximately two-thirds of federal expenditures during the emergency period and that the proposed increases in personal income taxes were substantial. He then outlined the detailed provisions the Treasury desired.

On May 19 he testified again to the same committee, this time focusing more on the rationales behind the overall approach in the administration's revised program and the specific increases. He zeroed in on the proposed changes to the excess profits tax and noted that recent polling indicated that the American public was willing to make sacrifices according to their ability.

By the beginning of June the Treasury Department had put together revised budget estimates that revealed that in order to adhere to the objective of paying two-thirds of the government's cost of the emergency out of revenues and one-third from borrowing money, the overall $3.5 billion target would have to be raised to $5.4 billion. After hearing from key congressmen that $5.4 billion was unattainable, Morgenthau accordingly withdrew adherence to that ratio. This development had the effect of intensifying the arguments with the executive sessions of House Ways and Means throughout the month of June.

On June 9 Stam raised the prospect of mandatory joint returns for husbands and wives, as the British did, which would deliver higher revenues. Morgenthau was concerned about a backlash from the public on that issue, so at his request, Sullivan ducked it before the committee for several weeks. The committee nevertheless voted in favor of it, but the Senate appeared to be balking. Sullivan informed Doughton that the Treasury would certainly have to adhere to the highest schedule rates if the joint return provision was rejected by the Senate.

A week later President Roosevelt called a conference on the tax issues. In addition to Sullivan and Morgenthau, Director of the Budget Harold Smith and Representatives Doughton and Cooper were present. FDR first satisfied himself that the excises did not constitute increased "nuisances" to taxpayers. He then asserted that if the excess profits tax provision as drafted by the House committee passed in its present form, both the Congress and the administration would be open to serious criticism. In particular he felt that the measure had negative political consequences in that it gave what amounted to a tax immunity to wealthy, prosperous concerns at a time when the administration was making great demands upon individuals and smaller corporations. He in effect told Doughton that Doughton had not done his job properly and that Doughton should reopen the issue in his committee. As the group exited the White House, Doughton spoke bitterly of his surprise and disappointment at the meeting. He blamed Treasury for causing the meeting and trying to reraise decided issues. He said he did not know what to do and that "this was the most unpleasant and unsatisfactory conference he had ever had."

Later on the same day, the president held a press conference in which he forecast heavier taxes the following year and a new tax bill every year during the emergency. The *Washington Post* on the 16th noted that there was not any mention of a boost in the $3.5 billion revenue target and that:

> Complete secrecy screened the move [the White House meeting and a rumored special meeting of the House committee] but speculation turned on possible revision of the committee's excess profits and corporate tax proposals into closer alignment with Treasury views.

Discussion apparently languished for almost two weeks. Then, on July 30, Sullivan was called out of a meeting on the Hill to an unscheduled conference with the president at the White House. Bell and Foley were also summoned. None of them knew why.

The president began by announcing that he had just had a telephone conversation with Speaker Rayburn about the mandatory joint return provision and that he wanted it out of the bill. He cited the number of divorces it would cause, and the opposition of the churches and the women of the country. He was personally going to write letters to Rayburn and Doughton to make known his opposition. He then went on to rail against the unnecessary complications of the income tax, saying:

> [H]e would like to have everybody who earned $750 pay so much tax, those who earned $850 pay so much, those who earned $950 pay so much. "In other words," he said, "a separate, distinct amount that everybody would know in advance was due. The trouble today is that too many people are earning money and not contributing to the Government." I then said that what he really wanted was a gross income tax. After a moment's hesitation he said, "That is just it." I then advised him that if he was interested in taking more people on the tax rolls this could be accomplished by lowering personal exemptions, but I was sure he didn't want that. He replied, "Of course I want that. I have been trying to get it for years but nobody will help me do it." I then stated that we had been battling for

three months to prevent a lowering of personal exemptions and we had been doing so because I understood that was his position. He then said that we did not understand his position. I advised him that it would be possible in the present bill to reduce personal exemptions but that it would not be possible to effect a gross income tax.

He reluctantly agreed to my suggestion and I asked him if he wanted the amount by which personal exemptions would have to be reduced to raise the three hundred million we would have on mandatory joint returns. He replied that he did. He then went into a discussion of excess profits, which he intended to open up again. Mr. Bell inquired if the President had any notion that he was going to be able to change excess profits at this session and the President replied, "No, but I am a woodchuck and I keep digging when there is a chance to dig, and since I have to write a letter on one phase of the tax bill I might just as well comment again on excess profits." He then went on to speak of the additional money that would be collected through a change in excess profits. I advised him that the change in excess profits could not be defended on that ground because the present system was capable of raising an increased amount of revenue.

The President then stated that he would like to see a tax which would tax all income above $100,000 at the rate of 99-1/2 percent. When Mr. Bell expressed his astonishment the President jokingly said, "Why not? None of us is ever going to make $100,000 a year. How many people report on that much income?" I replied that I thought about 1100 taxpayers reported income in excess of $100,000 a year.

He then discussed the form of the letter he desired and he asked that we write stating the opposition on mandatory joint returns and excess profits, omitting from the letter any reference to the position the Treasury had taken on lowering personal exemptions. He stated that he would also like some material on excess profits which would not be included in our letter but enclosed for use in his letter to Chairman Doughton. Mr. Bell said, "This is certainly going to be a bombshell." The President made no comment.

On our return to the Treasury [the group] worked on the composition of the letter until 6:30 p.m. Mr. Bell phoned the Secretary [who was at his farm in Upstate New York] and advised him of the situation, expressed his anxiety, and urged the Secretary to return. This the Secretary readily agreed to after calling the White House, asking for a postponement so he could have his day in court, and learning that he would have to be here by 9:30 tomorrow morning in order to see the President about this matter.

The next morning Sullivan, Bell, and Foley met the secretary at the airport and discussed the matter while riding to their offices in the Treasury Building. Thereafter Morgenthau met with the president, where the president asked for some slight changes in the Treasury letter, which were then incorporated.

Following the White House conference on the 30th, Sullivan attended a dinner at the Burning Tree Club, an exclusive golf club in Bethesda, Maryland, given by the full House Ways and Means Committee. Such social gatherings putting together people from both sides of the political aisle were commonplace in official Washington in that era. Dinners hosted by both Morgenthau and Sullivan served the same purpose of defusing ideological tensions. Similarly, Sullivan diary entries during the spring and summer of 1941 show that in addition to his work on the major tax bills, he handled numerous fiscal questions raised by the Navy and War departments. In that regard he dealt regularly with Secretary of the Navy Knox on contentious business matters yet also played golf frequently with Knox, and he and Priscilla had Mr. and Mrs.

Knox to their home for dinner on several occasions. Unfortunately, as the twentieth century wore on, such social intermingling that facilitated resolution of difficult issues would come nearly to a halt. Partisan divides on Capitol Hill and bickering among various agencies and departments of the executive branch would become more and more the norm.

During the first week of August, tensions on the tax bill were defused as the debate switched over to the Senate. Sullivan testified before the Senate Finance Committee on August 8. Since aspects of the president's suggestions had been included in a revised Treasury proposal, the emphasis of Sullivan's remarks was now on the rationale behind the legislation, focusing more on the need to defray defense costs and resist price inflation as well as the desire to create a more equitable distribution of the new tax burden.

The Senate worked on the bill throughout the month of August, and on the evening of September 4 Sullivan could report at a White House meeting that the Senate was expected to pass the bill the next day and that introducing further changes at that last minute would be unwise. Sullivan then worked with Senator Alben Barkley the next day to round up votes, and the bill was voted out of committee and passed by the Senate that afternoon. The House returned from recess and passed the bill on the 16th. In conference the same day, the House surrendered to the Senate on all major positions. The Senate approved the conference report the next day. On September 20 at Hyde Park the president signed into law the 1941 Revenue Act, the largest separate tax bill in the history of the United States (a levy of nearly $3.6 billion), to partly defray $25 billion of defense costs and lend-lease expenditures. Taken with preexisting law, the act imposed a total tax bill of $13 billion upon 1941 taxpayers. This was accomplished by permanently extending the temporary individual, corporate, and excise tax increases of 1940, increasing the excess profits tax by 10 percentage points (the top rate rose from 50 to 60 percent), and increasing corporate tax rates 6 to 7 percentage points (the top rate increased from 24 to 31 percent). Some excise taxes were temporarily increased (on alcohol, tires, etc.), and the personal exemption fell from $2,000 to $1,500 for married couples.

But the Treasury team knew that even the '41 bill would not be enough. On November 5 Sullivan and Morgenthau met with the leaders of House Ways and Means and proposed their 1942 tax bill, asking Congress to start work immediately on a program that would yield an estimated $4.8 billion through still higher Social Security taxes and a new income tax levy to be withheld at the source by employers from payrolls. The new measure was based both on the need to further finance the multibillion-dollar arms program and on the necessity to stave off inflation.

War

Following church on Sunday, December 7, 1941, John Sullivan drove slowly out Massachusetts Avenue to the Burning Tree Club. The air was chilly, but a warm sun assured that with proper clothing the golf would still be pleasant. The assistant secretary was in good spirits as he looked forward to a light lunch and the prospect of finding an enjoyable game.

At the luncheon table he was pleased to find a hearty foursome that had played in the morning but wanted to play another nine holes while the afternoon sun was still high in the sky. They invited John L. to play along with them.

It was an interesting group, all affiliated with CBS: Harry Butcher, CBS Washington vice president and soon to be General Eisenhower's naval aide; Jess Willard, manager of CBS's Washington facilities; Paul Porter, CBS Washington's outside counsel; and last but not least, Edward R. Murrow, famous for his broadcasts from Britain during the Blitz, which always began with the words "This is London," who had just returned from England.

As the now "fivesome" was hitting their drives on the tenth tee, a message came out for Murrow from Steve Early, President Roosevelt's press secretary, that Reuters was reporting that the Japanese had bombed Pearl Harbor. Dismissing the report as "very unreliable," Murrow proceeded to tee off with the others.

When the players reached the twelfth tee, a message came again from the clubhouse that John Sullivan was wanted on the phone. Sullivan told the courier to go and find out who was calling. On the next tee the courier came back and said Secretary

Morgenthau was trying to reach his assistant. The club's history records that:

> With a few appropriate remarks about government service in general and Secretary Morgenthau in particular, Sullivan betook himself to the Club House and the foursome continued. As they proceeded up No. 15 fairway, another courier came running to hand Butcher a match cover on the inside of which Sullivan had scribbled the following message: "Butch. Japs have bombed Pearl Harbor."

The remaining foursome immediately returned to the clubhouse and verified the report. It was recorded that Murrow sat down, deep in a locker corridor, put his hands to his face, and quietly wept. Later that evening, Murrow had supper with the president in the Executive Office, watching as the commander in chief took the first steps toward national mobilization.

* * *

Sullivan's job had just intensified immensely. He and Morgenthau agreed that the team at Treasury, particularly in the tax area, needed to be substantially enhanced. To that end, on December 12 Morgenthau named the eminent New York tax lawyer, Randolph Paul, as a special assistant reporting to Sullivan. Over the course of the next three years, Paul, who would became the department's general counsel in August 1942, until he resigned in March 1944, took up the reins on the detail work of the following three tax bills of 1942, '43, and '44, both fine-tuning the major steps taken in the 1940 and 1941 Revenue Acts and raising additional money as the expenses of war kept growing. Sullivan remained involved in that aspect in advisory and supervisory capacities, but he began spending more of his time in other areas of his wide-ranging jurisdiction.

At this point the Roosevelt administration's new revenue laws had created seven million new American taxpayers. Morgenthau feared that the government was reaching the limit of what revenue could be raised via increased taxes. On the day after Pearl Harbor, seizing on a comment from Undersecretary

George Buffington, Sullivan suggested to Morgenthau that "What John Barrymore can't do, maybe Mickey Mouse could," and that they should call Walt Disney for some help. With Morgenthau's blessing, Sullivan contacted Walt Disney, to see if Disney's studio could produce an animated cartoon film to help convince all taxpayers that it was their patriotic duty both to pay taxes and even to pay in advance. Walt Disney flew to Washington on December 17 at Sullivan's urging even though it was his wife, Diane's, birthday. He met with Morgenthau and "had dinner at Sullivan's house that evening, where [he] roughed out a scenario over martinis, and then phoned Diane to wish her a happy birthday. He signed a letter of agreement the very next day, promising to produce a film for not more than $40,000, which was less than the cost of a typical Disney short." Disney completed the film, titled *The New Spirit*, in less than four weeks. Sullivan sent Disney a letter of appreciation that said:

> I find it difficult to express to you my appreciation of what you have done to help us solve a difficult problem. I have never seen any type of picture that set out to do a particular job and which so completely accomplished its objective in an entirely effective way. How you were able to do this in such a short time is beyond my comprehension, but frankly I doubt if you could improve upon it if you had six months more time in which to do the job.

Disney launched a massive publicity campaign for the film, and a number of magazines printed promotional articles. Years later, in his autobiography, Disney praised Sullivan, but had no good words about how Treasury had otherwise handled the relationship—specifically, Morgenthau had attempted to micromanage the script (he wanted Mickey Mouse in it, not Donald Duck) and the directing of the film and ultimately, with congressional approval, refused to pay the Disney Studio the full bill for its extraordinary effort. While there was some legitimate question about how the bill was calculated, the reaction of the government was particularly egregious in light of the fact that "over 32 million Americans eventually saw the film at nearly twelve thousand theaters, and of these viewers, according to a Gallup poll, 37 percent said that the film had had an effect on their willingness to pay taxes, and 86 percent felt that Disney should make shorts for the government on other subjects." Much to his credit, Disney did in fact go on to make other patriotism-inducing films for other government agencies.

* * *

The Disney episode marked the beginning of Sullivan's new role as an all-around troubleshooter and sometime public advocate on numerous major issues for Morgenthau and the Treasury Department during the remainder of the war.

The first of these areas was war bonds. On April 30, 1941, President Roosevelt launched a nationwide sale of Defense Savings Bonds and Stamps, to be administered by the Treasury Department. When war was declared, the notes were thereafter referred to as war bonds. One of John Sullivan's jobs became to ensure that the American people bought as many bonds as they could possibly afford. Immediately, on the evening of December 12, he convened a secret meeting at his home with, among others, Chairman of the Federal Reserve Marriner Eccles, Director of the Bureau of the Budget Harold Smith, and the administrative assistant to the president, Lauchlin Currie. The purpose was to coordinate the administration's steps in regard to monetary policy, the savings bond campaign, and the timing of the new 1942 tax program. Eccles led off, espousing the necessity for restrictions on wages and prices to prevent taxes from increasing prices and his view that the people would not be willing to take a strong tax program until there had been some further inflation. Randolph Paul indicated that implementation of the collection-at-source tax effort should start soon, but in the end the group agreed that the tax program would wait until the bond campaign was stressed immediately.

On December 22, Sullivan informed Morgenthau that he had met with the budget director on a War and Navy departments proposal that legislation be enacted relieving defense activities from state sales taxation. Sullivan told the budget director that Treasury opposed the bill. Budget Director Smith was to present the policy difference to the president for resolution. The proposal would reverse a Supreme Court decision subjecting such defense activities to state sales taxes without exception for the situation in which the tax was on the purchaser and the United States was the purchaser. Sullivan told the Budget Bureau that Treasury's opposition was on the grounds that the bill would deprive the states of necessary revenues and interfere with Treasury's position regarding tax-exempt state securities. Acknowledging that some new legislation was essential to clarify the situation, Sullivan suggested that the federal government accede to state sales taxation in all cases, regardless of the legal incidence of the tax and regardless of whether the United States or the defense contractor was the purchaser of the commodities in question. Months later, after considerable wrangling, Sullivan's suggestion prevailed.

On Saturday, January 3, Sullivan gathered confidential information from the Office of Production Management concerning the availability of shipbuilding facilities and sources of funds to build new shipways. That evening and Sunday he worked with the Budget Bureau preparing the president's annual budget message. He continued to strongly oppose "value-added" taxes because they worked a disproportionate hardship on lower-class taxpayers, and battled at length with the White House concerning its overestimate of tax collections in fiscal year 1943 based on the upcoming new tax law. At another meeting the following Thursday, during a hearing at Ways and Means, Sullivan met, apparently for the first time, James Forrestal, the newly appointed undersecretary of the Navy.

In a speech to the Virginia General Assembly in Richmond on January 19, 1942, Sullivan said that the goal of the '42 tax bill was to make taxes so heavy that they "approach, but not reach, a point beyond which we cannot go without deadening individual initiative, dulling corporate management, encouraging extravagance and inefficiency and thus not only retarding our war effort but killing the goose that lays the golden eggs."

On January 24, 1942, Sullivan delivered to the Federation of Women's Clubs the first of many speeches urging Americans to pay their taxes on time and cheerfully to support the troops. A week later, he delivered a CBS Radio address with the same message. He did so again on March 9, 11, and 13.

On several occasions in December 1941 and January 1942, he met with members of the press, urging them to be careful during the emergency not to inflame differences of opinion within the executive branch and with the public.

On February 20, Sullivan obtained the agreement of Secretary of the Navy Forrestal and Secretary of War Robert Patterson that they had no objection to the marginal tax rate going to 90 percent (apparently on incomes over $100,000).

In April Sullivan was again in extensive discussions with the Navy and War departments regarding a list of the major war contractors and which ones had built the principal Army cantonments and largest bases in 1941. In May these discussions were expanded to possible renegotiation of defense contracts in order that the proper treatment could be given them for federal income and excess profits tax purposes. The same group met again in late May to gather information and instruct the states on the ways in which their laws and actions were impeding the war effort. In the tax collections area, he met with Justice Department officials regarding auditing of tax-exempt institutions.

On May 28, Sullivan testified before the Joint Committee on Internal Revenue Taxation on war profiteering—"particularly unpardonable attempts to escape wartime taxation." He later devised an Internal Revenue Bureau "working arrangement" to monitor and retrieve illegally gotten gains in that regard.

On June 14, he gave a vigorous address on the importance of purchasing war bonds before the combined United Nations/ Flag Day Rally in Chicago. He made another, similar one on July 9 in Boston.

Sullivan frequently walked or rode with Secretary Morgenthau all or part way to the office in the morning or back home in the evening. These walks and rides afforded Sullivan the opportunity to keep apprised of crucial aspects of his job and to assess the secretary's current thinking on important issues facing the department. July 3 was such a morning, and they walked halfway to the office and rode the rest, discussing a lengthy list of items from tax evasion to taxes on alcohol to the war bond effort.

Developing a plan to coordinate with the Justice Department in developing and supplying information to Justice in its efforts to combat subversive activities was the subject of a meeting in late August at the attorney general's office.

Sullivan spoke about war bonds on Labor Day, September 7, in Manchester, in Kansas City on September 16, on the 29th to the Washington Community War Fund Committee, and to the Community War Fund Drive on October 16. It was back to the subject of taxes in a speech in New York City on October 27 to the Savings Bankers Association; he then returned to war bonds on November 17 at the Waldorf Astoria before the Forum on Current Problems.

During October Sullivan also worked with Justice James F. Byrnes, currently director of the Office of Economic Stabilization with the White House, to develop regulations imposing gross salary controls on wages and with a cap of $25,000 on executive salaries. Byrnes announced the program on October 27. It fell to Sullivan to implement the regulations as they related to wages and salaries over $5,000. On October 29, he explained the new rules to the press and the public. Two weeks later his office issued detailed regulations to guide administrators and corporations in that stabilization program. Sullivan was compelled to spend substantial amounts of time dealing with the private sector's resistance to these new government rules.

In December he was consumed by the development of new regulations governing the renegotiation of Navy and Army contracts with suppliers, including extensive meetings with Forrestal and Patterson. This work continued through 1944, evolving into oversight after the regulations were issued. On February 10, 1944, Forrestal expressed his appreciation to Sullivan for his handling of matters in this area.

On December 9, 1942, Sullivan met with other key administration officials to discuss inflation controls, higher taxes, extensive rationing, and enforcement of price and wage ceilings. Chairman of the Federal Reserve Eccles and Ben Cohen from James Byrnes' office were among those in attendance, working on a program for submission to the president.

On December 14, he went to the NBC studio to make a transcript of a radio broadcast in support of the war bond program.

In February 1943, Attorney General Francis Biddle pressed Sullivan to fill an open position as a federal district court judge in New Hampshire. Sullivan told Biddle he could not accept the offer. He did not record his reason for declining, but it is not difficult to understand why: Sullivan was much too active a personality, particularly at the young age of forty-three, to sit still for the rest of his life in a judge's chair.

In 1943 Sullivan spent a great deal of time on the tax-collecting aspect of his job. This effort included compiling extensive data for submission both to the secretary and the White House as well as to the relevant Capitol Hill committees. On several occasions he testified at hearings of the Ways and Means Committee regarding this subject. He was in direct contact personally with Dr. George Gallup regarding Gallup polls of the public's willingness and ability to pay the new taxes and their understanding of the process and forms. Under Sullivan's leadership the number of tax collectors grew to thirty-five thousand. Tax collecting became the second-largest business in the country. Only the sale of war bonds, also part of John L.'s jurisdiction, topped it in dollar volume.

Regarding tax collecting, Sullivan appeared on the cover of *United States News* on March 12, 1943, and the inside story on him set forth a memo to the public describing the progress of the Bureau of Internal Revenue in its duties and the importance of everyone paying their taxes. He had touched on the same points in a speech to the Associated Industries of Massachusetts in November 1941. He revealed how much he enjoyed this part of his job when he commented in October 1943 that he kept his finger on the financial pulse of the country via the tax collecting process:

> You'd be surprised at how much you can learn from the tax receipts as they come in. . . . By the receipts on gas taxes, you know how much is consumed. By taking the income tax receipts for the various states and comparing them with those of past years, you find which sections of the country are prospering, and a lot of other things. . . . [N]early every activity of the Government cuts across my desk sooner or later.

He was also on Capitol Hill during this period seeking Congress's approval to continue the stabilization program and the Treasury's authority to devalue the dollar. Senator Barkley and others at first indicated that there was substantial support for the former, but there might be some difficulty in getting a continuance of the power to devalue. Sullivan proceeded to draft a memorandum for circulation on the Hill as to why the power to reduce the gold content of the dollar should be extended. Ultimately both provisions were approved.

At the end of May, Morgenthau asked Sullivan to focus more on supervising procurement issues. In this area, Sullivan supervised all U.S. government purchases of goods and services other than for the War and Navy departments, and about 40 percent of lend-lease materials. Morgenthau's request precipitated Sullivan's examination of the legal and practical issues, including deflation and inflation, that could follow the dumping of surplus materials by procurement after the war and the devising of a plan to ameliorate adverse effects of any such activity.

On June 11, an editorial in the *Washington Post* stated that the president was planning to announce at a press conference that he wanted to institute compulsory savings and to put Justice Byrnes in charge of the new program. Sullivan immediately called on Steve Early and informed him that such a new program would wreck the morale of Treasury's entire field force on the bond program, including between three hundred thousand to four hundred thousand voluntary workers. After consulting with Earl Godwin and other aides, Early and the White House capitulated to Sullivan's request to change that item in the press conference.

In mid-August, Sullivan was once again called on to resolve a dispute between Treasury and Colin Stam at the Joint Taxation Committee regarding Stam's request for internal Treasury memoranda. Sullivan met with Senator George and Congressman Vinson and devised a methodology to resolve the problem.

On September 8, 1943, Sullivan kicked off a third War Loan Drive at Union Station in Washington, complete with a galaxy of movie stars.

During 1943, Sullivan continued to give a great many speeches in support of the Treasury's war bond effort. One given in October in Chattanooga, Tennessee, included his recurrent theme:

Ten years ago, in December, 1933, there were over 25,000,000 people in over 7,000,000 households dependent upon work projects or direct relief. In contrast today, 26,000,000 people are setting aside a substantial part of their pay envelopes every week in the year for the purchase of War Bonds. Over 50,000,000 people have become investors in War Bonds. These savings constitute the greatest thrift program that the world has ever seen. I believe that the spread throughout the country of this practice of thrift contains tremendous social, economic and political implications for our national future.

In late 1943 and throughout 1944, Sullivan's attention was centered more and more on anticipation and resolution of issues that the country would face when the war ended. He coordinated with the Navy and War departments on a Joint Contract Termination Board that addressed these issues, and in December 1943 the board promulgated a uniform contract termination clause.

On December 29, he again reviewed the president's budget message and made numerous suggestions. On the same day he accepted an invitation to speak on NBC Radio on war bonds.

In January 1944, the administration formed a Surplus War Property Board, made up of representatives from State, Treasury, War, Navy, Justice, the Reconstruction Finance Corporation, the Bureau of the Budget, and several other agencies, to continue and expand the work begun by the Joint Contract Termination Board. Sullivan became a prime mover in the group throughout its meetings that year.

June dealt John L. another happy moment at home when second daughter Deborah was born on the 20th.

In the summer of 1944, Sullivan was still actively plugging the war bond effort, appearing in New York City's Central Park with Mayor LaGuardia and Secretary of War Patterson before three hundred thousand people.

Sullivan attended the July 1944 Bretton Woods conference in New Hampshire with Secretary Morgenthau, but there is no record of his substantive involvement.

By Labor Day, the attention of the nation turned once again to the upcoming presidential election. Sullivan made several speeches beginning with the New Hampshire State Democratic Convention in August. He assured Morgenthau that his talks would be entirely on the issues in the campaign and would in no way deal with Treasury policy. On October 3 he presented to the secretary for submission to the White House a detailed list of charges, with answers, that the Republican nominee, Governor Thomas Dewey of New York, might make against Treasury on the tax front.

* * *

A couple of Sullivan stories that occurred while he was at Treasury reveal his alertness to detail. The first happened as a result of his office, Room 288, overlooking the White House. One day in 1943 he had occasion to be at the White House and asked an assistant, "Where is the president? He must be out of the country." He had noticed from his office window that the president's flag was not flying as usual on its pole; by tradition that only happened when the president was out of town. Sullivan's question caused a big flurry, and the president's flag was immediately raised outside. In fact the president was meeting secretly in Casablanca with Churchill, and the staff at the White House had inadvertently forgotten to keep the flag up to hide the fact of the out-of-town meeting. The second story occurred when Sullivan noticed and brought to the attention of the president's security force that the number on the license plate of the president's automobile had long been 110, identifying precisely in which car in a cavalcade the president was riding. The security people immediately assigned that number to Sullivan and began rotating the plate on the president's car. Sullivan retained that license number as long as he lived.

A third tale reveals his irrepressible sense of humor. During the time Sullivan was at Treasury he was visited by the tax commissioner of the State of Connecticut, whose name happened to be the same as his—John L. Sullivan. Seizing on the opportunity for a little fun, the assistant secretary asked the Connecticut man to sit in his chair to greet his next appointment. The Connecticut man did so, and with a straight face introduced himself as the

Treasury's John L. Sullivan while our own John L. sat silently to the side on a couch. After a few minutes, to complete confusion on the second visitor's part, both Sullivans broke into laughter and admitted their mini plot.

While he was serving at the Treasury Department, Sullivan became acquainted with the then senator from Missouri, Harry Truman. During the late summer of 1944 Truman lived in the Sullivan house while Bess Truman was back in Missouri. Six weeks after Truman assumed office on April 12, 1945, Sullivan and Clark Clifford, a Washington lawyer then serving as an assistant to the president who would subsequently become Special Counsel to President Truman, arranged Truman's first relief from the rigors of the White House—a visit on May 26 to Burning Tree Club in Bethesda, Maryland, where he was made an honorary member of the club, delivered some short remarks on the awesomeness of his new tasks, played the "Missouri Waltz" and "Beautiful Ohio" on the piano, and engaged in a lively game of poker.

Harry Truman had become prominent during the war as chairman of the Senate Committee to Investigate the National Defense Program. Sullivan concurred with the general opinion that Truman had done a "superb job" in that capacity. As the Democratic convention in Chicago neared in the summer of 1944, a critical decision faced the party in light of Roosevelt's deteriorating health: the choice of who would be selected for their vice presidential candidate. Three people were in the running: Henry Wallace, who was the sitting vice president and wanted to remain, James Byrnes of South Carolina, and Truman. Sullivan's opinion was that "I think it was a case of God being good to America. Jimmy Byrnes would have made a good president, but I think Harry Truman made a better one." He added "I wasn't sorry to see [Wallace] leave. . . . [He had] fuzzy ideas [and] I don't believe . . . he really belonged."

Sullivan attended the convention and remembered:

> I got the word about 11 o'clock in the morning from Bob Hannegan that the President had decided upon Senator Truman. Believe it or not, in those days, I knew at least two-thirds of the delegates

from all over the country, and I promptly went to Mr. Truman's room, and I congratulated him and said I thought it would be nice if Mrs. Truman and [daughter] Margaret sat in the box at the head of the main aisle with me, and I would introduce Mrs. Truman and Margaret to as many delegates as came down that aisle, and I did that. Everybody wondered why I was stopping them and introducing them to Mrs. Truman and Margaret. About an hour later they found out.

Sullivan was also there when Roosevelt was later inaugurated on January 24, 1945, on the South Portico of the White House. He observed, "I hadn't seen him since the last week of the campaign, and both Mrs. Sullivan and I were frightfully shocked. There had been such a disturbing change in his appearance that we both felt that he was desperately ill."

* * *

Throughout the Sullivans' time in Washington, both during the war and afterward, the popular Sullivan was heavily engaged in the social whirl of the capital city. Once he was asked how he managed to survive the pace, and Sullivan replied, "I discovered early on that potted plants thrive on scotch and soda." Sullivan enjoyed being in the social, political, and media worlds of influential players, a fact that was always obvious to his family. When his daughter Deborah was a young girl, she became angry with him one time and shouted, "You're a nobody. You don't even know *Ed Sullivan!*" A few days later she was shocked to see the television celebrity walking up to their front door, and laughed. Just as at his office, John L. well knew how to defuse a family problem with humor and directness.

Priscilla Sullivan, by nature a private person focused on raising her children and partially on gardening, held up her end of the marital relationship by gracefully attending the many formal and informal events and receptions calling for the presence of a presidential appointee and his spouse. She was a voracious reader and was not hesitant to share her opinions on a wide variety of subjects within the family. Her principal outside passion was historic preservation. She was an active member of the Colonial Dames of America and devoted substantial amounts of time to Mount Vernon and Gunston Hall in Virginia and the Moffatt-Ladd House in Portsmouth, New Hampshire.

Three years after he left Treasury, on February 6, 1947, Sullivan was awarded the department's Distinguished Service Award and Silver Medal for services on behalf of the war finance program from 1941 to 1945. World War II had cost the United States $ 303 billion. Sullivan's work on five major tax bills had helped defray a portion of that amount, and the seven war bond campaigns in which he played a major role ultimately raised approximately $186 billion to finance the government during that period.

5

Assistant Secretary of the Navy for Air

During the 1944 presidential campaign, President Roosevelt easily outshone the humorless Dewey, particularly with his famous speech defending Republican "attacks" against his "little dog Fala." He was also helped by good news from the war in the Pacific: General MacArthur returned to Manila as he had promised, and the United States Navy destroyed the Japanese fleet in Leyte Gulf. The only question in the public's eyes was FDR's health, which he answered with vigorous campaign addresses in adverse weather. In the end Roosevelt won by a large margin. He carried thirty-six states with 432 electoral votes to Dewey's twelve and 99. John Sullivan sent the president a note of congratulations on attaining a record fourth term.

Sullivan resigned as assistant secretary on November 15, 1944, effective at the end of the month, in a letter hand-carried to President Roosevelt by Secretary Morgenthau, "because I had so many cases in New Hampshire that had been postponed and I had to clear them up," and citing that he had already extended his original commitment four times. He did not mention that perhaps he felt there was little more he could achieve at Treasury and a hoped-for presidential appointment to the Navy Department had not yet materialized. Earlier in the year he had resisted pressure from the New Hampshire Democratic Party to resign as assistant secretary and challenge Republican Senator Charles Tobey in November. He later wrote to a Chicago friend that:

The Senatorial thing didn't work out. Our Party broke up into four factions and each one proceeded to hammer the daylights out of the other three. All four factions were for me but I couldn't see any chance of getting anywhere unless the boys were together and that is just what they refused to do. Accordingly, I gave it a pass.

He then also declined an offer to become chairman of the Surplus War Property Board. He chose rather to turn to the task of reestablishing his private law practice and began preparations to open an office in Washington with a friend, Lawrence Bernard, Assistant General Counsel at the Treasury Department, and Jack Shea, Sullivan's own special assistant there. Then, on April 12, 1945, his plans were interrupted by an extraordinary and unique series of events:

On the day of the [President Roosevelt's] death, I was in the office of Basil O'Connor, who was the head of the American Red Cross. . . . The phone rang and Basil said, "It's for you."

I took the phone and this voice said, "Can you be at work at 8 o'clock tomorrow morning?"

And I said, "Who's this?"

He said, "Jim."

I said, "Jim who?"

He said, "Forrestal."

Whenever you talked with Forrestal, he never said "hello" or "goodbye," you were right in the middle of the conversation the minute you picked up the receiver. I said, "No, I can't be at work at 8 o'clock in the morning."

He said, "Be here at 8 o'clock Monday."

I said, "Wait a minute, Jim, what about?"

He said, "Haven't you heard from the president in the last 48 hours?"

I said, "No."

He said, "Did you fill out a blank check [i.e., tell the president he was willing to accept another position] when you left the Treasury?"

I said, "Yes, I guess I did."

He said, "Well, he's filled it in and we sent your nomination papers down to Warm Springs this morning, and they're going to suspend the rules of the Senate and you'll be confirmed tonight. Be here Monday morning."

I said, "Wait a minute, as what?"

He said, "Assistant Secretary of the Navy for Air."

So I told Basil what I was in for, and left and returned to the Waldorf and couldn't find any newspapers in the newsstand. I inquired why they didn't have any newspapers and they said, "Oh, stick around. There'll be another extra in a minute."

I said, "Another extra? What's happened?"

He said, "President Roosevelt died."

Well, that freed me of any obligation [a nomination lapses if the Senate does not act upon it while the president who sent it up is still in office] and I returned to Washington and started my own law firm.

Two weeks later I had a call from the White House asking me to see President Truman at 11:30. I went over there and he said he wanted to nominate me for Assistant Secretary of the Navy for Air. I assumed that he was making good on a commitment that his predecessor had made to me, and I tried to explain to him that he was under no obligation because the undertaking ran in the opposite direction. It was not a very satisfactory conversation for two minutes, because nobody bothered to tell Truman that Roosevelt had also nominated me for the same job. He didn't know that. [Nominated to the same post by two different presidents acting independently in the course of one month!]

I have been told that Mr. Roosevelt signed the document, that it was the last time he ever did sign his name.

Sullivan did show up the following Monday at the main Navy building on Constitution Avenue (subsequently torn down after the Navy moved to the Pentagon in September 1946), and threw himself into the new job enthusiastically even before he was confirmed or sworn in. He said "I immediately went over to the Navy, sort of incognito. I was to relieve Artemus Gates who was [still in the post Sullivan was to assume before moving up to undersecretary]. He was extremely helpful. He gave me an office, which was shared by a lieutenant commander and a WAVE [the Navy's WWII female corps, awkwardly named the "Women Accepted for Volunteer Emergency Service"], and to which office he sent all of the material I needed to study up for the job I was about to assume."

He made immediate arrangements to get into the middle of the war before it was over. He was finally confirmed by the Senate on June 20 and on the evening of the next day boarded a Navy plane and headed for the Pacific theater with Vice Admiral Aubrey Fitch, deputy chief of Naval operations for air, and the hero of the Battle of the Coral Sea. They traveled 21,291 miles by air and 4,900 miles by ship, conferring along the way with top Navy and Marine Corps leaders and with fliers and fighters from the ranks. He was with Admiral William F. ("Bull") Halsey's Third Fleet when it closed to within one hundred and thirty miles off Japan to make strikes against the main islands. Sullivan flew some reconnaissance patrols, but the brass said no when he requested to go on a bombing mission to Japan.

Because Artemus Gates had not yet taken over as undersecretary, Sullivan could not be sworn in before he left on the trip. In the Pacific he received word that Gates had moved up, so Sullivan was sworn in aboard the aircraft carrier USS *Shangri-La*, Vice Admiral John McCain's flagship, on July 2. After the ceremony he passed a sailor busily chipping paint. The young man called out after him, "Hi, John L.! How's the hook?" Sullivan recalled, "I nearly fell overboard, I was so surprised when the sailor turned out to be one of my old caddies, a grand boy, James ("Shorty") Morrisette of faraway Manchester." The sailor had remembered that on the golf course Sullivan had a reputation for hooking his tee shots. The two men shared a quick reunion as other sailors crowded around them.

The trip to the Pacific was a typical manifestation of Sullivan's thoroughness and his desire for firsthand information about the activities taking place under his command. He was impressed more than ever by the power and versatility of aircraft carrier operations. The importance to the nation of maintaining a strong Navy was forever burned into his psyche.

When he returned to Washington he immersed himself in the tough administrative aspects of his job including fighting for more special fuel oil for the Navy, overseeing postwar demobilization, and establishing a peacetime Navy.

Throughout his time in the Navy, Sullivan handled most of the matters on the Hill; he was his own Congressional liaison. He said that, "They [the people on the Hill] all knew what I had been doing at Treasury, and I had handled for five years the work with Congress, while representing the Treasury Department. The things I was working on in those days were tremendously important, so important that every member of the House and Senate in both parties was vitally interested in what I was doing, and I got to know almost all of them." He also pointed out that there was a big difference between the way Roosevelt had handled legislative matters relating to the Navy, which harkened back to when he had been assistant secretary of the Navy in World War I, and the way Truman handled them:

> Well, you see, President Roosevelt was President so long that all of the natural instincts of self preservation in the Navy atrophied. Whenever anything started to go wrong, somebody would call the naval aide who would speak to President Roosevelt, who would then call the chairman of the appropriate committee and inquire what he was trying to do with his (meaning Roosevelt's) Navy. It wasn't the United States Navy, it was Roosevelt's Navy, and he protected them all through the years. . . . So, when I got there there wasn't anybody who knew very much about Congress or cared that much about them.

As assistant secretary for air, Sullivan took advantage of every opportunity to plug the Navy and carriers in particular. In a speech on September 22, 1945, he declared that "aircraft carriers, 'the eyes and fists of the fleet,' were the deciding factor in the Pacific, and they will continue to be one of our most potent weapons until planes are able to fly around the world 'on a pint of something or other.'" He referred to the fast carrier task force as "the all purpose weapon."

The war soon came to a close. The Germans surrendered to Allied forces on May 7, 1945, and VE (Victory in Europe) Day was celebrated on May 8. Three months later, on August 6, in an effort to end the war in Asia without having to invade the Japanese mainland with an attendant massive loss of American lives, the United States dropped an atomic bomb on Hiroshima, Japan, followed by another drop three days later on Nagasaki. On August 14 the Japanese emperor capitulated, and Japan's formal surrender took place on board the USS *Missouri* on September 2 (VJ Day—Victory in Japan). Within two months, on October 24, the United Nations came into existence when the charter was ratified by a majority of the signatories.

Sullivan was about to become embroiled in the aftermath and consequences of the great conflict.

6

Under Secretary of the Navy

At the time he became assistant secretary for air, observers noted that Sullivan appeared destined to move up in the Navy hierarchy because he was well regarded by both Truman and Forrestal. His rise began less than a year later when he was moved up and sworn in as under secretary on June 17, 1946. Winning the job was not automatic. Edwin Pauley, a California oil man, was nominated originally, but his conflicting interest in tideland oil triggered opposition. David Lawrence, then a columnist for *The United States News*, questioned Pauley's competence when compared to Sullivan:

> In the same Navy Department at the present moment is an Assistant Secretary, John Sullivan, who has learned the ropes quickly and who has given much promise as the man who could take over the entire department. He used to be Assistant Secretary of the Treasury under President Roosevelt. He is a Democratic and an able lawyer, and he comes from New Hampshire, which is a state the Truman Administration, if politically inclined might well be cultivating. Why wasn't Mr. Sullivan selected? He, too, has qualifications of a political sort, and he is a man who has been confirmed before by the Senate for a post of the highest importance. Under his jurisdiction was the Bureau of Internal Revenue and

the supervision of other units requiring the services
of a man of unquestioned integrity.

Shortly thereafter Pauley's name was withdrawn, and Sullivan's name was sent to the Senate.

In attendance at Sullivan's swearing-in ceremony, along with his family, were two old Manchester cronies, his closest personal friend and police commissioner, Dr. (of dentistry) John F. County, and the city's chief of police, James ("Jimmy") O'Neil.

Sullivan had only been in office for three months when he became involved in a political squabble that further enhanced his standing with President Truman. It related to Henry Wallace, who had been appointed to be secretary of commerce after he was replaced by Truman as vice president.

Robert Patterson, secretary of war, and Forrestal, who was still secretary of the Navy, had been summoned to a meeting on September 12, 1946, at six p.m. in the office of Acting Secretary of State Will Clayton. In Forrestal's absence from Washington, Sullivan attended in his stead. Clayton called the meeting because he was concerned by a copy of an address that Secretary of Commerce Henry Wallace was to deliver in New York City that evening. The Wallace speech spoke:

> severely against any alliance with "British imperialism" and laid down a "soft" policy toward Russia that appeared to amount to a division of the world into two great spheres of influence and turning the larger over to the Soviet Union—it seemed to many that this represented a complete reversal of the entire course of the [Secretary of State] Byrnes' foreign policy. To make matters worse, Mr. Wallace had included the statement that the President had read and approved his speech; and when the reporters at the White House press conference on the 12th had asked the President about this, he contributed to the confusion when he gave them to understand both that he had read the whole speech and that he thought it exactly in line with the Byrnes' policies.

Sullivan also noticed that Wallace stated, "We are still armed to the hilt. Our excessive expenses for military purposes are the chief cause of our unbalanced budget." Sullivan immediately took charge of the situation. As described in a memorandum he wrote to Forrestal later that evening, he said, after determining that the speech was to be delivered at seven p.m. Washington time, "I asked him [Clayton] if he had protested to the White House and he answered in the negative. I then suggested that he call the White House and see if: (a) the speech could be stopped; (b) the White House could prevail on Secretary Wallace to delete the . . . sentence . . . in which Secretary Wallace stated that the president had read these words and said they represented the policy of his administration." The group immediately got on the phone and finally reached Charles G. Ross, the president's press secretary. The end result of the exercise was that Wallace could not be reached in time, and the speech was delivered. Byrnes insisted that either he or Wallace would have to go. "'You and I,' he messaged the president on the 19th, 'spent fifteen months building a bipartisan policy. We did a fine job convincing the world that it was a permanent policy upon which the world could rely. Wallace destroyed it in a day.' Next day the president announced that he had asked for Mr. Wallace's resignation." Sullivan's effort to warn the president in time to avert the confrontation had fallen short, but Truman undoubtedly learned later of John L.'s alertness and loyalty.

The Greek-Turkish Military Aid Bill, the Truman Doctrine, and the Marshall Plan

By the end of 1946, fueled by warnings from the likes of Great Britain's Winston Churchill, Clark Clifford at the White House, and George Kennan at the State Department, the attention of the United States' defense efforts turned to the Soviet Union. Both Forrestal and Sullivan shared a high degree of concern about the Russian threat. At Forrestal's request, Sullivan directed Admiral Nimitz to analyze and report on how many carriers it would take to defend the Mediterranean in the event of war there. Nimitz's reply was that it would require four to sixteen of the giant ships plus support vessels. Nimitz stated:

> If we throw away [the Navy's air power], we shall
> be restricted to an air campaign of strategic bombing
> only from one base. . . . I am of the opinion that
> to permit our strategic thinking to evolve about a
> single concept in which air conducts . . . strategic
> bombing from the United Kingdom will be very
> unsound. . . .[M]aintenance of the Mediterranean
> will be the keystone to any successful war against
> Russia. . . . We have the capability; it can be valu-
> able; we should not give it away.

It was no secret that the Soviet Union had long sought access to
the warm water ports of the Mediterranean. In the first weeks of
1947 it appeared to Secretary of State George Marshall that the
Russians were on the verge of achieving that goal by extending
their Communist regime via a takeover of Greece and Turkey.
Greek guerrillas were aligning themselves with and receiving
assistance from the (as it turned out, Yugoslav) Communists, and
Soviet troops were massing along the Turkish border. In February
Britain announced that it could not meet its commitments in those
two countries.

In early February, President Truman called John Sullivan
over alone to the Oval Office and asked him to take three days
and do nothing else but sound out both houses of Congress on the
prospects of enacting the legislation. Sullivan did so and reported
back that:

> [E]verybody on the Hill had been very gracious, but
> they said the country was tired of military appro-
> priations, and for me not to batter my head against
> a stone wall because I'd never get anywhere with it.
> President Truman then asked me if I personally felt
> such a bill was desirable. I answered in the affirma-
> tive. If you recall, at that time, Italy and France were
> on the verge of going Communist and Yugoslavia
> was one of the brightest jewels in the Communist
> crown, and if we lost the east end of the Mediterra-
> nean, namely Greece and Turkey, there would be no
> barrier to stop Communism from going over into

Africa, which was very ripe for subversion at that time.

> When the President learned that I was very much in favor of the enactment of this legislation, he said, "Well, John, you and I have taken an oath of office, and it's time we lived up to it. Are you willing to batter your head against the stone wall that they referred to?" And I said, "Yes." He said, "Let's get on with the drafting of the bill."

On February 27, the president called a meeting of congressional leaders to his office where first Secretary of State Marshall and then undersecretary Acheson made stirring presentations pressing the urgent need for aid to Greece and Turkey. Senator Arthur Vandenberg of Michigan, the key Republican chairman of the Committee on Foreign Relations opined that if a strong presentation was made to Congress, both the House of Representatives and the Senate would give him the money he requested.

Marshall instructed his undersecretary, Dean Acheson, to draft an aid bill for submission to Congress and then headed overseas. On March 7 the president called Acheson (Marshall was in Moscow on an investigative visit) to his office and told him of his decision to go ahead with an aid bill.

On March 12 the president appeared before a joint session of Congress and delivered a dramatic speech that set forth what became known as the Truman Doctrine. He asked for, and got, $300 million in military and economic aid for Greece and $100 million for Turkey. More broadly and importantly he said, "I believe that it must be the policy of the United States to support free peoples who are resisting attempted subjugation by armed minorities or by outside pressures. I believe that we must assist free peoples to work out their own destinies in their own way. I believe that our help should be primarily through economic and financial aid which is essential to economic stability and orderly political processes." The president had just announced to the world that America would come to the aid of any country, not just Greece and Turkey, that was threatened by Communism. He had laid the basis for the policy of deterrence and containment that would be followed by all of his successors during the Cold War.

During the next three months the president's emissaries, led by Acheson and including Sullivan, fanned out over Capitol Hill promoting the doctrine and seeking the specific aid that Truman had requested, Finally, in May the Congress approved the Greek-Turkish aid bill by a wide, bipartisan margin. Truman signed the bill on May 22, and American aid was soon on its way to the Mediterranean. Truman was later quoted as saying that in light of the prevailing American mood of isolationism, selling the economic and military assistance plan for Greece and Turkey was "the greatest selling job ever facing a President."

That same month George Marshall returned from a meeting of the Council of Foreign Ministers in Moscow that had broken down over the issue of German reparations to the Soviet Union. Marshall felt that Stalin was delaying resolution of this and other outstanding issues in order that the Communist parties in Western Europe could take control of the deteriorating situation there. He determined that something dramatic was called for; the result, following discussion and coordination with President Truman and Dean Acheson, was the Marshall Plan that he articulated on June 5, 1947, at the Harvard University commencement. He proposed that the United States donate billions of dollars to rebuild Europe's economy, assuring that Communism could not take hold in those countries.

As a result of the Marshall Plan's huge success, the European economies began to recover, and Communism was once again contained. Sullivan later stated that, "I think the Marshall Plan received a very cordial welcome from the Houses of Congress, probably because of the spade work that had been done on the Greek-Turkish Military Aid Bill." Others have spoken more strongly, concluding that the Marshall Plan would never have passed if it had not been preceded by the Greek-Turkish measure, making the Congress receptive to the idea of large expenditures for military and economic aid overseas so soon after World War II.

The Unification Debates

In November 1943, General of the Army George C. Marshall had issued a call for the merger of the Navy Department and the Department of War when the war was over. His proposal triggered what became known as the unification debates, and led to the later passage of the National Security Act of 1947. That act created what was called the National Military Establishment, which in 1949 became the Department of Defense, an independent U.S. Air Force (previously part of the Army), the National Security Council, the Central Intelligence Agency, and combined the three military services into the Defense Department, with each of their secretaries reporting to the secretary of defense, thereby technically depriving them of their Cabinet status.

Prior to his new appointment Sullivan had made clear his view that the Navy should remain separate from the rest of the military. In a Navy Day speech on October 27, 1945, he had said that it was:

> . . . unthinkable [that all the military forces of the nation should be entrusted to] any single individual [with either an Army or Navy background]. Co-ordination between the Army and Navy can be perfected while maintaining the advantages of the present system. America will suffer far more from the termination of competition and free expression from the War and Navy departments than it ever did from imperfect co-ordination.
>
> Early in its history, America recognized the value of competition. We early learned that lack of competition was a serious sociological, as well as an economic threat. Hence there was developed in this country that great body of anti-trust laws and decisions which assured for America in the business and industrial world one of our greatest assets. Yet there are those who today seek to persuade us that in the military field, unlike every other phase of human endeavor in the country today, monopoly is desirable.

He repeated these views in a speech to the American Legion convention in Chicago on November 17. Previously, on August 30 he had made it clear that in his view the atomic bomb did not make the Navy obsolete.

Sullivan could not have appreciated at the time that these public expressions were the beginning of his involvement in a debate that would be pivotal in his career.

Even before passage of the National Security Act, the Army Air Corps generals argued that strategic bombing, particularly with atomic weapons, was the only decisive element needed to deter or win any future war. Therefore they began lobbying to build a large fleet of U.S.-based long-range strategic heavy bombers, beginning with the B-36.

The Navy leadership immediately challenged the Air Force. They argued that the aircraft carrier had been dominant in the Pacific theater during the war and that to initiate the use of nuclear weapons against an enemy's population centers was immoral. The admirals proceeded to request that Congress authorize a fleet of supercarriers, the first of which would be the USS *United States* (CVA-58). The projected carrier, at sixty-five thousand tons, would be the largest ship ever built, have a speed of thirty-three knots, and accommodate four thousand men. Its estimated cost was $124 million.

Independent analyses would also show that the Air Force arguments against the carrier were fallacious:

> At a time when there was no defense against it, strategic bombing with atomic weapons could achieve great destruction at small cost in terms of men and resources. But the Air Force was [not only] deficient in intercontinental planes that could deliver the bombs, [it] could not rely upon the use of foreign bases, and lacked the power to absorb or divert atomic attacks upon the United States. It had also to depend upon the other services for forces needed in any kind of war, destroy enemy submarines or a widely dispersed fleet, or mount an amphibious

invasion. Thus it could not undertake the invasion
and occupation needed to consummate victory.

Sullivan insisted on satisfying himself on the ship's merits. He conducted his own review of it, including lengthy, tough questioning of his admirals' corps. Only then, in the face of massive Air Force publicity against the supercarrier, did he support its construction.

The Secretary of the Navy (soon to be Secretary of Defense) James Forrestal, after obtaining the approval of President Truman, authorized construction of the *United States*.

7

Secretary of the Navy

*I*n the waning days of 1947, after John Sullivan became secretary of the Navy, George Dixon, a reporter for the *Washington Times-Herald*, recorded a story told to him by Sullivan about his Navy experience that is an indication of the ingenuity he demonstrated during his career:

> John L. Sullivan gave me a very John L. Sullivanish look out of his fighting Irish pan and said: "Did you ever hear how I got to be Secretary of the Navy?"
>
> I said, ingratiatingly, that it was undoubtedly through pluck, perseverance, and unremitting service far and above the call of duty.
>
> "Nuts!" snapped Mr. Sullivan. "I wasn't going to give you any of that old guff. Few people know it, but I really got my start towards this job in the first world war when I was a bluejacket.
>
> "I was about as lowly a bluejacket as you can be. Around that time a batch of high-minded idealists began babbling about 'war aims.' The result was that a 'war aims school' was set up at Yale and we had to take time out from fighting the war to attend it. As nearly as I could figure the purpose of this war aims school was to teach us how to recite Wilson's 14 points backwards.

"My immediate superior at this school was a tough master-at-arms, or 'Jimmy Legs.' He seemed to think we were at war just so he could ride hell out of John L. Sullivan.

"At that time, our greatest naval hero was Adm. William Snowden Sims, the man who taught the Navy how to shoot. He was the sailor's god.

"I was walking down the street one day, wondering how I could murder this 'Jimmy Legs' and get away with it, when I saw a big picture of Adm. Sims in a store window. I went in and bought it. Then I sent it to a friend of mine in New York with certain instructions.

"About a week later the picture came back inscribed as follows:

"'To John L. Sullivan—with very fond wishes for a fine naval career for my favorite nephew. Uncle Billy.'

"I left it on my bunk for the 'Jimmy Legs' to see. He did—and I never had any more trouble with him.

"Although I never met Adm. Sims, and certainly can claim no relationship, his picture continued to serve me nobly. The other day, after the President announced my appointment, I received a note from my old bunking mate, Christopher Columbus Baldwin, now by decree of fate, a colonel in the Army. All Christopher Columbus wrote was:

"'I see Uncle Billy's picture is still working for you!'"

It was a good story, typical of Sullivan. Perhaps Uncle Billy's ghost did provide John L. with some continuing good luck, but it was Harry Truman and James Forrestal who were responsible for Sullivan becoming, in September 1947, the first "unified" secretary of the Navy.

John Sullivan's tenure as secretary, from September 1947 to April 1949, was marked by an overriding dilemma—how to coalesce (1) his efforts to save the Navy from damaging diminution due to demobilization following World War II and threatened obsolescence as a result of a widespread belief that the Air Force was all that was needed to preserve the nation's security so long as it had enough atomic bombs for B-36s to deliver, with (2) supporting at the same time the unification of the three military services as mandated by President Truman. Resolution of this dilemma would present challenges he most certainly could never have anticipated.

During the initial year of his term, Sullivan was assisted in his efforts to meld these competing objectives by his predecessor, Jim Forrestal, now John L.'s boss as secretary of defense.

James Forrestal

James V. Forrestal was an extraordinary American. He was born in Matteawan (now part of Beacon), New York, on February 15, 1892. His father, who had emigrated from Ireland in 1857, ran a construction company and dabbled in politics. His mother's mother had also come from Ireland. They were Roman Catholics. Young James was an amateur boxer while in high school, after which he worked for local newspapers for three years before attending Dartmouth College and then Princeton University. He was an editor of *The Daily Princetonian* before leaving college just before graduating. The reasons for his sudden departure remain unclear, but were apparently a mix of academic and financial concerns. He then went to work in New York for the investment firm William A. Read and Company in 1916 and stayed with the firm until 1940. During World War I he took a leave of absence to join the Navy as an aviator. Upon returning to the firm after the war, he became a partner in 1923 and president of the company, then renamed as Dillon, Read Co., in 1937.

After the war, Forrestal began doing some publicity work for the Democratic Party in Dutchess County, New York. One of the politicians he helped to win election was a neighbor by the name of Franklin D. Roosevelt. On June 22, 1940, Roosevelt appointed him as a special administrative assistant, and soon thereafter nominated him to be under secretary of the Navy, a post he held for four important years during World War II, handling procurement contracts, tax and legal matters, and liaising with other agencies.

He gained a reputation as a highly effective administrator while mobilizing industrial production.

Forrestal became secretary of the Navy on May 19, 1944, when his boss, Secretary Frank Knox, died of a heart attack. John Sullivan served as his assistant secretary for air and then his under secretary until September 18, 1947, the day after Forrestal was sworn in as the first secretary of defense, when Sullivan, on Forrestal's recommendation to President Truman, became secretary of the Navy. At the same time, Stuart Symington became secretary of the new Air Force, and Kenneth Royall was sworn in as secretary of the Army. The four men headed up what was at first called the National Military Establishment. Only Forrestal was a member of the president's Cabinet, but the National Security Act initially afforded him only three civilian assistants on his own direct staff. He chose three superbly qualified men to fill those slots: John Ohly in charge of policy and as liaison with the Department of State, Marx Leva to handle legal issues and congressional relations, and Wilfred McNeill to oversee fiscal matters.

Four years earlier Sullivan had played a part in setting the stage for Forrestal's own career in the Navy and at Defense. Sullivan much later described to a historian the circumstances when he first became acquainted with Forrestal:

> My father and I had been very good friends with Frank Knox who was Forrestal's predecessor as Secretary of the Navy. One Sunday in [1940] Secretary Knox phoned me and asked me to lunch with him aboard the *Sequoia*, the Navy yacht. When I arrived at the *Sequoia*, he asked me several questions about Forrestal and told me that President Roosevelt had agreed to create the office of Under Secretary of the Navy, and wanted Secretary Knox to take a look at Forrestal. We agreed that after lunch Knox would pretend to take a nap for an hour and I would have a chance to talk alone with Jim. Shortly thereafter Jim arrived, we had lunch, Secretary Knox went below, and Jim and I talked for about an hour. I liked very much his style, his directness, his candor,

> and when Secretary Knox came above again I gave
> him the silent signal with a nod of the head and
> went below. When I came on deck an hour later Jim
> had been offered the job by Knox and accepted.

The story is testament to the high regard Knox and others had for Sullivan's ability to evaluate the attributes and character of other people. A similar example of Sullivan's ability to spot and promote good, qualified people and the way in which he quietly wielded his connections behind the scenes related to the selection of Robert Dennison, captain of the battleship USS *Missouri*, as Truman's naval aide:

> He was a first-class fellow in every way. On that
> job, it's very important that the wife of the Naval
> Aide be simpatico with the President's wife. Mrs.
> Sullivan invited Mrs. Truman, and maybe eight or
> ten other women, to tea one afternoon, and Mrs.
> Dennison was one of the invitees and didn't know
> why she was there. She was there for Mrs. Truman
> to look her over, and Mrs. Truman liked what she
> saw and Bob got the job.

Fighting to Save the Navy While Implementing Unification

The National Security Act was passed by the Congress on July 26, 1947. It went into effect at midnight, September 17, just hours before Sullivan was sworn in as secretary of the Navy at noon. Truman thereby got his wish for a single defense department, but only after months of wrangling among the services over the details. And it would take many more months and even years in some respects before the final organizational aspects were resolved. Still, particularly controversial issues remaining were naval aviation and the independence and continued existence of the Marine Corps.

Once the National Security Act was passed, Sullivan put aside his initial resistance to unification of the services. He and Forrestal at that point appeared to be of like mind on the way in which the act should be implemented. In sum, they both interpreted it and began to take action on it as requiring only *coordination* among the services as opposed to melding them into a *single, unified* body. Within the context of that interpretation, Sullivan declared, "This thing [unification] is going to work." A Navy historian concluded that notwithstanding his reservations about all-out unification, Sullivan's "diplomatic talents smoothed the wrinkles out of the troublesome transition to the unified National Military Establishment."

At the time Sullivan took over as secretary at the Navy Department, it had, overall, a personnel of 339,000: 12,000 in Washington, 283,000 spread over the rest of the country, and 44,000 overseas. He dove into the management of this vast organization with his usual thoroughness and fervor. He spent the first two months immersed in the great mass of paper that crossed his desk.

> Thereafter he delegated certain tasks to his civilian executive assistants and thus kept himself free to reach policy decisions in performing his primary task, policy control, or the administration and control of his department as a whole, including the functions of public relations; legislative affairs; morale; the nomination, removal, and reassignment of the principal civilian and military men in his department; and liaison with the other services and with the Department of State. Meanwhile he asked the General Board of the Navy to study and report to him on the probable nature of warfare in the next ten-year period and also on how to bring the Navy to the highest point of effectiveness so that it could contribute to the warmaking capability of the nation within the framework of the National Security Act.
>
> While Sullivan assigned naval representatives to the numerous national security agencies, he also interested himself in revising the code of military justice; planning for the exploration, conservation, and development of the mineral resources of the subsoil and seabed of the continental shelf; in getting rid of racial discrimination in the Navy; in supporting soil conservation methods on land

owned by the Navy; and in establishing a Naval Arctic Research laboratory at Point Barrow, Alaska. Because he firmly believed that those who had a hand in deciding, influencing, or implementing naval matters should understand how the Navy operated, he invited Forrestal, Symington, and various congressmen to sea cruises on carriers or cruisers during winter-time exercises in the Caribbean; corresponded with many congressmen, businessmen, and labor leaders; invited various business and community leaders to attend a Navy Civilian Orientation Course to be held at Pensacola, Florida; and also asked the presidents, chief executive officers, and professors of Naval Science to attend an orientation course in the Naval Training Program, also given at Pensacola.

Even at the start of his tenure, however, managing the Navy Department did not insulate Sullivan from the country's major foreign policy issues. On September 30, within two weeks of taking office, Sullivan directed Admiral Nimitz to send a task force to operate in the Gulf of Oman and the Arabian Sea through the summer of 1948 in order to familiarize the Navy with the situation there and to put pressure on the Russians by a show of force in the Middle East.

Postwar budget pressures made it difficult to preserve a strong Navy. Senator Harry Truman had served on the Appropriations and Military Affairs committees from 1935 to 1945 and had also been chairman of the Special Committee to Investigate the National Defense Program. He concluded that the military services had "unquestionably squandered billions of dollars" and that he "knew . . . that Army and Navy professionals seldom had any idea of the value of money. They did not seem to care what the cost was." Later, in his *Memoirs*, he said that when he became president:

It was inevitable that many pressures were brought to get me to approve larger appropriations. This was particularly true of the military. The military frequently brought pressure to force me to alter the

> budget which had been carefully worked out to achieve balance with the other needs of the government and our economy as a whole. If, for example, the three departments of the military were allocated a total of nine billion dollars, the Army, the Air Force, and the Navy would usually ask for an equal three billion no matter what their actual needs might be. Such an arbitrary distribution obviously did not make sense. I therefore insisted that each service justify its demands and prove why it was entitled to an equal division. The services were unable to do this and soon began to break away from the old practice that everything had to be divided into three equal parts. I compelled the three branches to be specific and exact about the requirements they considered essential. Every single item in the military budget had to be justified to me and the Secretary of the Treasury.

Truman apparently never saw the inconsistency between these words and his own overall approach at the White House level. When he did become president and was faced with mounting civilian governmental needs and the billions of dollars needed to fund the Marshall Plan, Truman adopted a practice of providing for the needs of the military only by giving them what was left over after first deducting everything else from projected revenues. While the final wartime budget, in fiscal year 1946, was $45 billion, for 1947 it was only $14.5 billion, and for 1948 it was to be even less at $11.25 billion, with the Air Force and the Army getting $6.7 billion and the Navy $4.4 billion.

In a later interview, Sullivan cited a specific example of how he carefully answered the president's directive:

> In the fall of 1947, my petroleum people told me that it was likely that we were going to have a very severe winter in the Middle West and along the Atlantic seaboard. President Truman had ordered a ten percent cut against all budget items, and accordingly the Navy had lost thirty million dollars for the

purchasing of petroleum products. I called in the heads of the big oil companies and they disputed the fact that there was any possibility of a shortage of oil in the Chicago area or on the northeast coast. My petroleum people were very sure there was going to be trouble, and I went to the President and put the question to him. He suggested that I call in the heads of the big oil companies, and I replied that I had already done that. I assured him that if he would restore the thirty million dollars taken out of our appropriation for petroleum products, I would top off every oil tank along the Atlantic seaboard; and if we did have a very bad winter, as our people were predicting, we would be able to mitigate the distress throughout the area.

By the middle of January, the following year, it was quite apparent that the Navy prediction had been correct, and I called in several of the New England governors, and my Under Secretary, John Kenney, worked out a contract with them whereby the Navy would lend the state agencies oil, which was to be returned in amount and kind by the middle of June. Of course, the Navy couldn't sell them oil because if we did the proceeds would go into the general funds of the Treasury.

When the word got around that we were taking care of the New England states, the governors of New York, Pennsylvania, New Jersey, Maryland, Virginia and South Carolina, all came in and executed similar contracts. This oil, of course, was used to heat hospitals and state institutions, and if we had not had that oil, it would have been a very rough winter indeed.

Incidentally, by the 15th of June, all but one state had returned the same amount and kind of oil, and the last one made good before the 1st of July.

Also to save money, Sullivan closed the Navy's West Coast lighter-than-air stations, put them in caretaker status, and shifted their activities to the Atlantic Fleet and the East Coast.

Although such efforts were helpful in meeting the new White House fiscal demands, Sullivan's main challenge was fitting the new supercarrier into the budget. In a November 7, 1947, letter he wrote that "I concur that the building of such a ship is essential to the maintenance of our sea-going air power." He thereby committed himself to seeking funds for the ship. On November 13 he telephoned Budget Director James Webb, who agreed that the new National Security Act did not require the Navy secretary to clear construction of the supercarrier with the other service secretaries or the secretary of defense.

The battle among the services for funds was paralleled by an inextricably related and ongoing dispute over the particular roles and missions that each of the services was to assume. On October 13 Fleet Admiral Chester Nimitz, the chief of naval operations, wrote to Sullivan (about the Army, before the Air Force was up and running as a separate entity) that:

> It has been made clear by repeated public discussion that the Army believes that the Navy should have all the ships with no aircraft and no troops; that the Army should have all the troops; and that the Air Force should have all the aircraft. The Navy believes that it should retain its present organization with particular reference to naval aviation, including its reconnaissance, anti-submarine and naval air transport components, and also the Marine Corps. It is surprising that this matter should be reopened at this time since the question was settled unmistakably by the Congress in the National Security Act of 1947.
>
> With respect to amphibious operations the Navy adheres to the concept to which there has been repeated agreement, that it should control the naval and amphibious phases of overseas operations and the Army should control the shore phases of such

operations. In simple language the Navy should be in control of amphibious operations until the troops are established on shore. The Navy agrees that the whole must be under a unified command.

Behind the general expressions under this heading there is apparent the thought, which has been stated publicly by many individuals in the Army, that navies are obsolete and that the size of the United States Navy should be reduced. In the planning activities it is obvious that there is an Army view to the effect that as a preliminary to future planning the naval establishment should be reduced, starting with naval aviation and the Marine Corps. Here again it would appear that this matter has been resolved by the decisions of the Congress. . . .

The Navy viewpoint is that the qualifications for naval personnel are different from those for Army personnel, that life at sea is different from life on shore, and that each service should procure and train its personnel in such a manner as to achieve maximum efficiency.

Without going into details, I feel it is necessary to comment that one of the obstacles to complete harmony between the services is a feeling in the Navy that the Army has not considered itself bound by the various agreements reached before the War, during the War and since the War. The Navy believes that agreements are binding until terminated by agreement. Likewise the revival at this time, within less than a month from the date on which the National Security Act became effective, of the Army concept that the naval service should not have the resources necessary for a balanced combat task force appears to indicate unwillingness to accept the decision of the Congress relative to naval aviation and the Marine Corps."

A major aspect of this dispute broke open when, almost immediately after Forrestal and his service secretaries assumed office, a blue-ribbon panel created by Truman and headed by Thomas K. Finletter, a New York lawyer, began hearings in September through November to study and recommend a national policy on civil and military aviation. In the public hearings there was an assumption that the country's emphasis in future wars would be on aviation and the atomic bomb. However, in the closed sessions the Air Force and the Navy battled over the size and nature of that air power and which service should control it. Symington led forcefully, demanding 988 heavy bombers including the B-36, as well as 5,881 additional planes, a mix of light and medium bombers, fighters, transports, trainers, and others.

Sullivan was taken aback by Symington's temerity, but shrewdly outlined a plan whereby naval aviation would be built up by "evolution" rather than "revolution." He requested only that Navy air be commensurate with the Navy's overall mission. He emphasized that it had been proved that the country's new jet planes could operate well from aircraft carriers. The first successful flight of a jet off and back on to a carrier took place on July 21, 1946, and "On May 5, 1948, the first all-jet fighter squadron, comprised of sixteen FH-1 *Phantoms*, qualified for carrier duty."

Sullivan lost a strong aide when Admiral Nimitz, his CNO, retired from active duty on December 17, 1947. As he retired, the popular hero Nimitz left with Sullivan a paper entitled "The Future Employment of Naval Forces." In the paper Nimitz reviewed how Navy air and sea forces had combined to bring victory in both theaters in World War II. He then outlined how, in the future, Navy ships and planes would be used defensively and offensively from carriers, coordinating with the Air Force to carry the war to the enemy safely away from the American mainland. Sullivan cannily released the Nimitz paper during the first week of January 1948. He beat Finletter to the punch; the New Yorker's Air Policy Commission made public its report on January 13. The Finletter report largely dismissed the utility of naval aviation.

Symington replied to the Nimitz paper in the *Saturday Evening Post* and attacked Nimitz's conclusions. That story was followed by a leaked memorandum written by Admiral Daniel

Gallery stating that, "It is time right now for the Navy to start an aggressive campaign aimed at proving that the Navy can deliver the atom bomb more effectively than the Air Force can." Sullivan reiterated that the Navy had no intention of intruding into the Air Force's domain of strategic bombing. He got Nimitz to sign a statement that he did not agree with Gallery and then reprimanded Gallery. Sullivan was doing everything he could to defend the Navy while at the same time avoiding an open confrontation with Symington. Privately he may well have shared the view of his under secretary, John Kenney, who regarded Symington as a man who pretended to be Forrestal's friend but was "repeatedly disloyal" and "in the front row of world-class double-dealers." Sullivan was provoked sufficiently to tell Symington privately that the Air Force had demonstrated an "immature attitude," that it should give "more cool and profound consideration to national security problems," and that "its attacks on the Navy were really attacks on the National Security Act."

As a successor to Nimitz as chief of naval operations, Sullivan recommended to Truman that the president appoint Admiral Louis Denfield, a 1912 graduate of the Naval Academy who had commanded a battleship division supporting the Okinawa landings in the Pacific in World War II and was currently commander of the Pacific Fleet. Truman appointed Denfield to a two-year term. Denfield selected Rear Admiral Arthur Radford, the Navy's senior aviator, as his deputy.

Forrestal, after obtaining Truman's approval, convened a meeting with the Joint Chiefs of Staff at Key West, Florida, from March 11 to 13, 1948, for the stated purpose of defining military roles and missions. The service secretaries were not invited. In his diary record of the meeting, Forrestal noted, "The Navy is to have the Air necessary for its mission, but its mission does not include the creation of a strategic air force." To the Air Force he made it clear that peace would be achieved only through the coordinated work of the full military establishment, not through the atomic bomb or any other single agent. Strategic bombing was labeled as primarily an Air Force function, but it was also a collateral function of the Navy and Marine Corps. The Navy should not be prohibited from attacking any targets necessary for the accomplishment of its mission. Another Navy function was "amphibious training of all forces as assigned for joint amphibious operations. Further, in reporting to Truman later in the month, Forrestal added that "Navy not to be denied use of A-bomb" and that "Navy to proceed with development of 80,000 ton carrier and development of HA (high altitude) aircraft to carry heavy missiles." Truman later approved of the Key West Agreement via Executive Order No. 9950, issued on April 21, 1948.

Suffice it to say that Sullivan was very happy later to learn that the Key West Agreement approved a supercarrier. He announced formally to the Navy on July 14 that he would follow the agreement and the follow-on functions paper as his guide to support the National Security Act. In the interim, on March 25, he fired a public broadside at those who would curtail the Navy, warning that submarines "not belonging to any nation west of the iron curtain" had been sighted in American waters.

On June 24, 1948, in response to a deutsche mark currency reform initiative by the Western powers that threatened the emergence of a recovered German state and extended to the western sectors of Berlin, Stalin and the Soviet Union blockaded all road and rail lines into Berlin across the hundred and ten miles of their occupation zone. Previously, on March 31, Sullivan, Forrestal, the other two service secretaries and the Joint Chiefs of Staff had met at the State Department to consider the options if the Soviets denied the Western nations access to Berlin. On June 21 they met again at State to help decide whether the United States would fight or opt for a different course. General Lucius Clay, the United States military governor in Germany, in turn called upon Air Force General Curtis LeMay to break the blockade by flying eighty tons of supplies a day into Berlin with C-47s and C-54s. Navy tankers were called upon to carry across the Atlantic the additional tons of aviation gasoline that would be needed. By the end of the year the Allies were supplying forty-five hundred tons of supplies a day, more than was required even for the coal needed for heating during the frigid German winter. During one twenty-four-hour period the next spring a record 1,398 flights went into the city, at a rate of one landing every minute. Finally, in mid-May, Stalin relented, the blockade was lifted, and the land routes were reopened.

The result of the successful effort back home in the States was that in the eyes of the public the Air Force had enhanced its position in its debates with the Navy.

On August 20 to 22, 1948, Forrestal, the Joint Chiefs of Staff, and their aides met at the Naval War College in Newport, Rhode Island, to make an appraisal of the capabilities and cost of present and future weapons and other key issues relating to strategic warfare. As at Key West, the service secretaries were again not present. Rather than confronting these issues, the conference sidestepped many of them. A main example of this that turned out to benefit the absent Sullivan was that the Air Force, in the person of General Carl Spaatz, the first chief of staff, reversed its position and suddenly agreed that "the Navy should be equipped with carrier-launched atomic bombs that could be utilized to attack strategic targets." It turned out that Spaatz had learned that the United States would shortly have an abundance of atom bombs, so that he could bypass the tough question of whether there was a true military need for duplicating the strategic bombing function. Forrestal, showing signs of fatigue, simply went along with the logrolling compromise.

In May 1948 a long-time Princeton friend of Forrestal, Ferdinand Eberstadt, was named to lead a committee task force to study the National Security Organization under the Hoover Commission on Organization of the Executive Branch of the Government. In response to the Eberstadt committee's questions, Sullivan stuck to the service roles and missions set forth in the National Security Act as interpreted by the Key West and Newport conferences. Sullivan's civilian special assistant Henry G. Beauregard, a member of the team preparing the presentation to the committee, challenged the proposition that strategic bombing alone could win a war on historic, economic, moral, and diplomatic grounds and emphasized the need of a sea-based air capability. He concluded that "air should be an integral part of the Navy (this is the guts of the case). . . . When it is necessary to puncture the [Air Force's] extravagant claims, the tone should be almost paternal toward boyish over-enthusiasm."

The committee report, completed in November but not forwarded to Truman until January 1949, concluded that the National

Military Establishment "was not soundly structured and was expensive." The committee recommended that the office of the secretary of defense needed significant strengthening, including the appointment of an under secretary, the Joint Chiefs of Staff should have a chairman, and that the defense secretary alone, not the service secretaries, should be on the National Security Council. The committee also disparaged the unseemly battle over whether the Air Force should have seventy air groups as an example of "a service program making national policy rather than national policy being implemented by a service program." When Beauregard later asked Forrestal's assistant whether the Navy's presentation was effective, he was told that the Navy had been too brusque in referring to the Air Force. "Beauregard replied that the Navy had not asked to testify, that it had been invited to speak 'fully, freely and frankly,' and that it should include the issue of naval aviation. 'How could one discuss whether the Navy should transfer its aircraft carriers and aircraft to the Air Force without comparing the efficiency of Air Force bombers with that of carrier aircraft?'" he asked.

The National Security Council created by the National Security Act of 1947 was a committee comprised of the president, the secretaries of defense and state, and the three military service secretaries. Its sole purpose was to advise the president; consequently it had only a skeletal staff. Sullivan felt that it was not particularly significant as a committee per se in the early years because few meetings were held and those were attended by too many assistants advising their bosses. The council was more effective via the medium of separate conversations among its members, including separate discussions directly with the president by each member. Thus, although Sullivan did not enjoy Cabinet status, as both a formal and a practical matter, via the NSC he had access to the president on a direct one-on-one basis.

Sullivan's view was that the State, War, and Navy Coordinating Committee, established in December 1944 to coordinate the postwar policies of the three departments, was a much more effective vehicle than the NSC as a means to correlate foreign and military policy. Although as a general proposition, he was not a "meeting person," much preferring serial one-on-one chats as a means of arriving at solutions quickly, he did feel that the SWNCC (pronounced "swink") meetings were productive to solving problems. (Undoubtedly he felt that way because the three representatives—Dean Acheson from the State Department, Robert Patterson from the Army, and Sullivan for the Navy—were all strong, decisive men who attended regularly and limited attendance by subordinates.) The SWNCC coordinated the policies of each department, and after receiving the approval of the Joint Chiefs of Staff, the coordinated result became the policy of the government. While originally established at the assistant-secretary level, by 1945 secretaries held the weekly meetings. The Subcommittee on the Far East was formed under SWNCC to draft a plan for the occupation of Japan. Two of the major policy statements produced by SWNCC were the United States Initial Post-Surrender Policy for Japan and the Reform of the Japanese Governmental System. The SWNCC was terminated in 1949 when the National Security Act was amended.

* * *

In 1947 and the early part of 1948 James Forrestal was pulled into the raging debate over whether the United States, the UN, and other member countries would support a separate Jewish state in Israel. Forrestal took the position that from a national defense perspective such a step was not in the country's interest. The military was concerned both that the Arab states would cut off the oil supply and that the Jewish fighters could be defeated by the Arab armies and the United States could be dragged in to save them. Whatever the merits of this position, Forrestal was immediately crucified in the press by Zionist interests in America. Drew Pearson and Walter Winchell wrote particularly vicious and often distorted pieces attacking him. President Truman ultimately rejected his point of view and supported establishment of Israel.

To add to the pressure on Forrestal, Truman, to the surprise of many after the election, still insisted that the defense budget for fiscal year 1950, then already under review, be capped at $14.4 billion. The services initially wanted $30 billion, and trying to the best of his ability Forrestal could not get them to budge below $23.6 billion. Symington was sticking to his demand for seventy air groups.

Sullivan struggled to meet Budget Director James E. Webb's guidance for the Navy. In order to preserve construction of the supercarrier *United States*, he cancelled the contracts for all ships not 20 percent completed, leaving thirteen ships still being built. He transferred the $337 million thus saved to the carrier. He also stopped conversion of a battleship and a cruiser. He used the $308 million thereby saved to build four fast-submergence submarines and an antisubmarine vessel, to modernize one carrier and one submarine, and to build a limited number of prototype ships for experimental purposes. He also submitted to Forrestal a draft paper labeled "Balanced Defense Forces," that Forrestal accepted, pointing out that the increase from fifty-five to seventy air groups that Symington wanted would cost up to $18 billion. Truman went along with this reasoning and sent an overall $14.2 billion request to the Hill, ignoring Forrestal's request for consideration of two higher levels. Symington, however, went around even Truman and convinced the House to give him the seventy groups.

Sullivan went to the Hill before a subcommittee of the Senate Committee on Appropriations on February 16, 1949, to support the president's defense budget for the upcoming fiscal year 1950. His testimony was summarized as follows:

> [Sullivan] noted that the budget cut was acceptable only "because of the overriding necessity for a military budget consistent with the needs of our national economy. . . ." He knew that about $21 billion was going toward the European recovery program and that peace had not been restored to the world. Yet by showing the flag, particularly in the Mediterranean, the Navy was helping to further peace and stability. Until international agreements were obtained that guaranteed peace, "we cannot discard our weapons, desert our responsibility, and leave in jeopardy our far-flung occupation forces overseas." Nor must we forget that, rich as we were, we were a "have-not nation" with respect to various strategic materials that came to us by sealanes that must be protected in time of peace as well

as in time of war. "We intend that within the screen of naval power if need be, and under the umbrella of air protection, those cargoes will always be able to move. In short, these considerations explain in part why we cannot abandon our naval strength, and why we cannot predicate our naval needs on a mere relative comparison with the navies of other powers."

Among questions asked of Sullivan was one by the chairman, George H. Mahon, of Texas: "It has been said, and there is a popular belief, that the Navy to some considerable extent has served its usefulness as a fighting weapon. I say a 'popular belief.' There is a popular belief that the atom bomb and the long-range airplane have sort of made the Navy obsolete. . . . In the fiscal year 1950 . . . how effective and useful and necessary would the Navy . . . be to the United States?"

Sullivan pointed to a world globe nearby, noted that 70% of it was represented by water, and retorted: "I would say the Navy would be more important, and would be more useful, and more ready than it has ever been at the outbreak of any war in our history," adding that because of the curtailment of the British Navy the American Navy was more important than ever before.

Were not aircraft carriers "sitting ducks" for land-based aircraft? asked Senator Harry B. Sheppard. Sullivan replied that in World War II, one third of the forty-two carriers were sunk by land-based aircraft, the others succumbing to carrier planes, submarines, or naval surface gunfire. When Sheppard wondered whether carriers could be defended against high-flying aircraft, Admiral Radford, who accompanied Sullivan, replied affirmatively, adding, "We feel no hesitancy in stating that our fighters today can take care of any high altitude attacks that will come at us with the planes in existence and the

> planes that we have projected in the future can take
> care of anything that comes at us that is planned
> for that type of operation." When Sheppard per-
> sisted in his questioning, Sullivan asserted: "I think
> a good deal of our difficulty comes from the enthu-
> siasm of single-weapons experts. I do not mean to
> address this against the Air Force, because we have
> in the Navy people who are so enthusiastic about
> their own particular specialty that they always have
> to be kept in bounds."

Sullivan thus skillfully pointed out the weaknesses that would result from the passage of the prospective 1950 budget while at the same time adhering to his support for the president.

On March 10, Drew Pearson reported that at a meeting at the White House with the president, Forrestal, and the other service secretaries, Sullivan stated a number of objections to the pending Armed Forces Unification Bill, including in particular the provisions that diminished the autonomous power of the secretary of the Navy. Pearson also wrote that Sullivan was reported to be a choice to replace John Snyder as secretary of the Treasury.

The budget fight tore at Forrestal's self confidence and led him to believe that he no longer enjoyed the president's support. Furthermore, by this time he was admitting to himself that the gradualist approach to unification that he had pursued simply was not working. As his biographers noted:

> Forrestal now believed five changes were needed:
> (1) to convert the anomalous "National Military
> Establishment" into a single executive department,
> (2) to provide the Secretary of Defense with
> unequivocal power to exercise authority and
> control over all the armed forces, (3) to create the
> position of Deputy of Defense to serve as alter
> ego to the Secretary, (4) to make provisions for a
> larger and stronger OSD staff, and (5) to create the
> position of Chairman of the Joint Chiefs of Staff, at
> a minimum to preside over the JCS and to focus
> their deliberations.

Based on these beliefs, Forrestal forwarded recommended amendments to the National Security Act to the president. In a message to Congress Truman pressed for their passage and on August 10 Public Law 216 incorporated them. But for Forrestal personally the legislation came too late.

Sullivan, along with others working closely with Forrestal, began to notice in the fall of 1948 that the defense secretary appeared to be exhausted and under tremendous pressure. The signs of mental breakdown were becoming apparent. Sullivan recalled that "Very early in October he began issuing me contradictory orders and from then on he went downhill, and very fast."

Because of Forrestal's erratic behavior and his growing differences with Truman's views, on January 11, 1949, Truman met with Forrestal and informed him that he intended to ask for Forrestal's resignation and replace him with Louis Johnson of West Virginia. On March 28 he was relieved by Johnson. His tenure had been historically significant, but relatively short—only eighteen months. His emotional tailspin continued, and on April 2 he was admitted to Bethesda Naval Hospital for psychiatric analysis and treatment, publicly for "nervous and physical exhaustion." On May 22, at age fifty-seven, he committed suicide by leaping from a kitchen window on the sixteenth floor of the hospital. The country was shocked. Letters of sadness and condolence arrived from throughout the world. John L. Sullivan issued a statement mourning "the passing of this distinguished public servant" whose achievements had "earned him the admiration of all Americans." Recognition of Forrestal's life and accomplishments would continue for months and years.

8

Nuclear Navy: The Decision to Build the USS Nautilus

At one fifty-five in the afternoon of December 3, 1947, Secretary Sullivan and Vice Admiral Robert B. ("Mick") Carney, the deputy chief of Naval Operations, hurried down the E-Ring hallway from Sullivan's office in the Pentagon to his big conference room. A historical decision was scheduled for two o'clock. When the two men entered the conference room a large group of flag officers stood and snapped to attention.

Even before the end of World War II, visionaries in the United States Navy had begun to think and talk about the possibility of nuclear-powered warships, particularly submarines. The wartime subs were severely limited: their diesel engines were excellent on the surface, but had to depend on battery-powered electric motors when submerged, which meant much slower speeds. Under the surface the boat was also completely dependent on its periscope to ascertain its own or an enemy's position. Recharging the batteries with the diesels when they resurfaced could take as long as six hours. The only real solution appeared to be nuclear power, which could create a "true" submarine capable of operating at high speeds for extended periods below the surface and requiring only a single propulsion system.

While Fleet Admiral Ernest King and his successor as chief of naval operations, Pacific war hero Chester Nimitz, both took early steps to promote research to investigate its possibilities, nuclear propulsion in 1945 had few advocates and even those admitted that its development appeared to be far in the future.

From 1946 to 1947 several naval officers nevertheless stepped forward to advocate and take the initial steps toward an all-out program to build a nuclear reactor that could power submarines. Foremost among those was Captain Hyman G. Rickover, who was then working at the Bureau of Ships facility at Oak Ridge, Tennessee.

The difficulties facing Rickover and his like-minded colleagues were monumental, ranging from gaps in basic research and organizational mismatches to bureaucratic infighting. To make matters worse, the top people at the Atomic Energy Commission, which President Truman had established in July 1946, were asserting their own territorial rights over all nuclear projects, and they failed to perceive the importance of a new, reliable reactor to the Navy. They mulled for months over different types of reactors for different purposes. The commission was populated by research physicists rather than practical engineers, and they foresaw a time period for physical completion of up to twenty years. Rickover wanted it done by the mid-1950s. But the believers among his engineers faced high hurdles in the areas of shielding, materials for construction, reactor controls, coolants, and heat-exchanger equipment. And even within the Navy, many high-ranking officers, most of them surface-ship types, had a preference for developing nuclear fission for weapons, not for ship propulsion.

Notwithstanding his own prickly personality, Rickover possessed heightened political instincts. As progress bogged down in the fall of 1947, he determined to "go over the top" for support. First, he drafted two memos, one for Admiral Nimitz to Secretary Sullivan, and the second from Sullivan to Defense Secretary Forrestal, approving the project to build a nuclear-powered submarine. He then enlisted the aid of two World War II submarine heroes who had both been awarded the Navy Cross—Captain Elton W. Grenfell and Commander Edward L. Beach (later the author of the popular book *Run Silent, Run Deep*). Those two prepared a supporting memorandum dated October 31, 1947, that was signed by Rear Admiral Styer, assistant chief of naval operations. On December 5 Nimitz, a sympathetic submariner himself, forwarded the secret Styles memorandum to Sullivan. This presented a major decision for the secretary, who was aware that the admirals' corps overall was split right down the middle on the issue.

Sullivan had studied all the paperwork on the issue intently and listened to all points of view at great length. The purpose of the meeting in the afternoon of December 6 was to deliver his decision.

Sullivan waved the admirals and other top brass—about sixty in all—to their seats and sat himself at the head of the table. As was his habit, he wasted no time. After slowly scanning the faces—most notably Nimitz, Denfeld, Carney, Spruance, Radford, Parsons, and Mills, as well as the others—he said simply and clearly:

> Gentlemen, for some weeks now you have plied me with the arguments for and against building the nuclear submarine. At this time, I must confess to you that I don't know whether Captain Rickover is right or wrong. However, I am sure of one thing: the country cannot afford to run the risk of not building the submarine and then learning later that it works. Accordingly, I have decided to support construction of the vessel. I am going to sign out to Admiral Nimitz and Dr. Bush at the Defense Research Board two memos that Mick will now distribute to you. As you may see, they are marked top secret. I expect full cooperation and effort from all of you in this matter. Thank you. Good day.

Sullivan rose and strode briskly back to his office.

Secretary Forrestal agreed with Sullivan's decision. On December 8 Sullivan named the Bureau of Ships as the Navy agency to develop the submarine, along with the Office of Naval Research.

Later in 1948, when the Atomic Energy Commission, apparently in some organizational disarray, resisted the program, which was designed to be a joint effort between the AEC and the Navy, Sullivan again entered the fray, firing off a letter to Forrestal protesting the AEC inaction. Rickover was able to use the Sullivan letter to force AEC reorganization and participation and to consummate private contractor relationships with General Electric and Westinghouse to clarify their roles in the development of the nuclear reactor.

In his annual report for 1948, Secretary Sullivan observed:

> The potentialities of atomic energy and its naval applications are limited only by imagination. Even rudimentary guided missiles present a difficult defense problem which will require many new techniques. Developments in submarines have indicated that a true submersible, i.e., a vessel that can operate indefinitely while completely submerged, is not beyond the realm of practicability. With seventy percent of the earth covered by water and with the advantages of concealment and difficult detection afforded by that water, it is possible that a future conflict might involve as many battles under the sea as on the surface.

The project resulted in the building of the USS *Nautilus*, which was launched at the Electric Boat shipyard in Groton, Connecticut, on January 21, 1954. Mick Carney, by then chief of Naval Operations, delivered the main speech in which he praised both the ship and the newly promoted Admiral Rickover. John Sullivan, now a private citizen, and his wife, Priscilla, attended by special invitation of the chief of naval operations. Mamie Eisenhower cracked the bottle to christen the ship, and the ship's first captain, Commander Eugene Wilkinson, took charge of the remaining construction work on the vessel. It cast off for its first sea trial on December 30, 1954. As the ship headed down the Thames River out into Long Island Sound, the signalman on the sub blinked out to the escort ship the historic message—"Underway on nuclear power."

Immediately the *Nautilus* began to set numerous records— cross-Atlantic speed records completely underwater, a trip to the North Pole, depth records, and many others. All of these have since been eclipsed by more sophisticated follow-on nuclear submarines. A total of 198 have been launched and put to sea since that cold, eventful day in 1954, and the Navy's nuclear submarine

Left: Patrick Sullivan, JLS's father and personal hero, 1918.

Below: Dartmouth college newspaper announces that undergraduate JLS wins election to mythical office of "Mayor of Hanover," 1921.

THE DARTMOUTH

ELECTION EXTRA

VOLUME XLII   HANOVER, N. H., SATURDAY, MAY 14, 1921   NOON EDITION   5 CENTS

SULLIVAN IS MAYOR

Representative of the People Receives Majority Vote of Hanover Townspeople, Defeating Andy Nicholson, Conservative Candidate—Will Assume Office at once at Simple Inaugural in Arts Room

EDITORIAL

The choice of the people has been indicated. When John L. Sullivan, elected mayor of the municipality, takes oath of office 14 minutes from now, Hanover will be sure that it has chosen capably and gloriously.

Too much cannot be said against that majority of Hanover townfolk who fight to push through such a man as Andrew B. Nicholson, blue law fiend, steader extraordinary, and reformer plenipotentiary. Too much cannot be against this representative of the B. Butler, who by his support of Nicholson, dragged the fair name of his session in the dust of disrepute.

On the other hand, too little can be said for those new and worthy members of Sullivan's candidacy was honest, fearless, and without taint of money. Too little can be said of Sullivan himself, that mighty, towering specimen of all that is good in American politics.

Sullivan will be a mayor who will fear neither man nor Smith girl. He will act with directness, with character, and with strength. He will place the position of mayor where it has never been before—on a paying basis, and he will see that this paying is done in the right way.

Sullivan is good; he is noble. In entrusting to his care the proprietorship of the chieftain's gavel, the citizens of this municipality have done the best and only thing that they could do.

Both Mr. Sullivan and the great majority of citizens who swung his way

NICHOLSON IS GAME

DEFEATED CANDIDATE TAKES BEATING STOICALLY

HONORED BY VICTORIOUS RIVAL

WILL BE OFFERED PLACE IN THE NEW MUNICIPAL GOVERNMENT

As the tide of the battle was decisively turning in Mayor-elect Sullivan's favor, Andrew B. Nicholson, the defeated blue law candidate, despondently, though bravely, turned to THE DARTMOUTH reporter at his side, declaring, "The king is dead! Long live the Mayor!" and "Viva la Hanover." He smiled and sat down, wearied and worn after his long hard fight for the premier hon-

JOHN L. TO PITCH FIRST BALL IN TODAY'S GAME

Successful Candidate Will Hand Keys of Hanover to Penn. Captain— May Be Unable to Attend Concert

John L. Sullivan, representative of the people, was elected mayor of Hanover over Andrew B. Nicholson, Conservative, this noon, by a majority vote of the townspeople of Hanover. The announcement of the result followed a day

THE NEW EXECUTIVE

Butler immediately began to bespeak the gathered mob's favor in behalf of his man, but he was interrupted by the arrival of the Sullivan chariot. Sullivan wore also conventional costume, and bore upon his head the one specimen of opera hat obtainable at local haberdashering institutions.

Sullivan was accompanied by his two

A NEW DEAL FOR NEW HAMPSHIRE

JOHN L. SULLIVAN
A DEMOCRATIC GOVERNOR
To SUPPORT ROOSEVELT

Fellows-Fitzpatrick Co. Manchester, N. H. ROBERT C. MURCHIE, Chairman Democratic State Committee.

Campaign poster—JLS runs for governor of New Hampshire, 1934.

Getting to the golf course during World War II gasoline shortage.

Top photo—In Washington: Senator Gerald Nye, JLS, insurance official Vincent Saccardi and William Dolph of Radio Station WOL in horse-drawn surrey on way to Burning Tree Club, May 1943.

Bottom photo—In New Hampshire: former Mass. Governor A.T. Fuller, former N.H. Governor Huntley Spaulding, JLS hitch ride to Abenaqui Golf Club, July 1943.

Top photo—Navy Secretary Frank Knox (l.) and Assistant Treasury Secretary JLS (r.) lead American Legion parade in Manchester, N.H., Labor Day, 1943.

Bottom photo—SECNAV (right rear) and Mrs. Knox (second from left in front) host JLS (third from left in rear) and Mrs. Sullivan (third from left in front) and other New Hampshire friends at party in Washington, January 1944.

| Burrough | Sherman | Blandy | Denfeld | Farber | Conolly | Radford |
| Ramsey | Nimitz | Forrestal | Sullivan | Snyder |

Top photo—JLS being sworn in as Assistant Secretary of the Navy for Air by Vice Admiral Aubrey Fitch aboard the USS Shangri-La, July 1, 1945. Vice Admiral John McCain, behind Fitch, looks on.

Bottom photo—Navy General Staff meeting with SECNAV Forrestal and Assistant Secretary JLS, January 11, 1946.

JLS deplanes on to USS Shangri-La *following reconnaissance patrol off Japan, July 1945.*

JLS on becoming SECNAV, September 1947.

Top photo—JLS speaking at commissioning of USS Coral Sea, *October 1, 1947.*

Bottom photo—JLS and Forrestal testifying before Senate Subcommittee, November 11, 1947.

Top photo—JLS receives Medal of Merit from President Truman, January 27, 1948. Left to right, Patricia, Charles, Truman, Priscilla with Deborah, JLS.

Bottom photo—Defense chiefs meet before Senate Armed Services Committee to urge Congress to strengthen nation's armaments, March 28, 1948. Left to right: Forrestal, Royall, Spaatz, JLS, Bradley, Denfield, Symington.

Captain Denison, White House Naval Aide, SECNAV JLS and President Truman at Army-Navy baseball game and crew race, May 1948.

Top photo—JLS confers with President Truman aboard the presidential yacht Sequoia,
May 1948.

Bottom photo—JLS fishing off New Hampshire coast, August 1948.

SECNAV JLS (right) with tuna fish caught off Portsmouth, New Hampshire coast, August 1948.

Top photo—JLS, a low-handicap golfer himself, presents the Abenaqui Invitational Cup to Art Butler, one of New England's all-time premier players, August 1948.

Bottom photo—JLS acknowledges gathering at colorful Navy ceremony as he leaves Pentagon following resignation as SECNAV, May 24, 1949.

Unfinished aircraft carrier United States (CV-58) lies in dry dock at Newport News Shipbuilding, Virginia, May, 1949.

Top photo—JLS with President and Mrs. Eisenhower, c. 1954.
Bottom Photo—USS Nautilus *at sea, c. 1955.*

JLS escorts President and Mrs. Johnson from church, c. 1965.

force has been instrumental in every one of the nation's major military crises.

Years later, in the mid-1960s, when Admiral Rickover, who was sharing a dais at a Navy dinner in Washington with John L., was introduced as the "Father of the Nuclear Navy" he rose and pointed to Sullivan and said, "That man is in fact the true Father of the Nuclear Navy." It was a very unusual and uncharacteristic accolade coming from Rickover, secure by then on his own historic pedestal in recognition of his years of effort. But it was a nice gesture that Sullivan forever appreciated.

9

"Dewey Defeats Truman": The 1948 Presidential Election

*T*he story of Harry Truman's unexpected come-from-behind win over New York Governor Thomas Dewey in the 1948 presidential election has been told many times; the famous picture of Truman exultantly holding aloft the *Chicago Daily Tribune* headline— "Dewey Defeats Truman"—is an iconic news photo in American political history.

The campaign and election were indeed remarkable. In the spring of 1948 public opinion polls all showed that Truman's popularity had dropped to 36 percent, down dramatically from the 70 percent he had enjoyed immediately after taking office. But he felt strongly that "there was no doubt as to the course I had to take." Principally he was concerned that he had to finish much "unfinished business" on both the domestic and international fronts that President Roosevelt and he had begun. The turnaround and eventual victory in November can accurately be said to have been achieved almost solely as a result of his own hard efforts. Even obtaining his party's nomination proved to be difficult. First there was a movement to draft the popular General Dwight D. Eisenhower. Then Henry Wallace, former secretary of agriculture and the vice president during Roosevelt's third term, mounted a challenge under a Progressive Party banner. And finally, at the Democratic convention itself, Strom Thurmond, the governor of South Carolina, bolted and left with a large group of Southern delegates to run separately as the "States' Rights Democrats," also labeled the "Dixiecrats." But when Truman rose to give his acceptance speech at two o'clock in the morning, he was well received when he characteristically "gave 'em [the Republicans] hell" and forced them back for a special session of Congress where he emphasized that they could not deliver on their political promises.

Truman did not kick off his campaign until Labor Day, and on September 17 he began an extended railroad "whistle-stop" tour that would eventually cover 31,700 miles and require his delivering 356 speeches. Twelve to fifteen million people gathered along the way to hear and cheer him. He later recorded in his *Memoirs*:

> My one-man crusade took effect. The people responded with increasing enthusiasm as the day of election neared. I never doubted that they would vote for me, although my advisors were still not optimistic and the polls continued to hack away at my chances of getting elected.

On the eve of the election the president slipped away from his home in Independence down to Excelsior Springs, Missouri, about thirty miles northeast of Kansas City. He went to bed before seven p.m. and slept until midnight, when he awoke to listen briefly to the radio broadcast of H. V. Kaltenborn. He then slept until four a.m., when he rose and learned from Kaltenborn that he was over 2,000,000 votes ahead. He then returned to Kansas City, where at ten-thirty he received a concession telegram from Dewey. The final count was 24,105,695 votes carrying twenty-eight states and 304 electoral college votes to Dewey's sixteen states and 21,969,170 votes. Thurmond garnered four southern states with over 1 million votes. Wallace also had over 1 million votes, but he carried no states.

Sullivan's role in that campaign was limited and strictly behind the scenes. In December 1947, the New Hampshire Democratic National Committee member Harry Carlson had announced that he intended to sponsor a slate of candidates in the March 9, 1948, primary pledged to President Truman for a new term and Sullivan for vice president. Sullivan discouraged that effort before the primary. As he later stated in an interview, ". . . I had an understanding with President Truman that the Navy was nonpartisan and hence I did not make any political speeches whatever. I did travel around the country on Navy business." He never made any references to the political situation during his speeches, but his mere presence on the road during the campaign was certainly interpreted by the voting public as positive support for the president's efforts. The muckraking columnist Drew Pearson later took an untrue potshot at Sullivan when he wrote that Forrestal was a "Cabinet Judas" and "Dewey's friend," and described Bernard Baruch (a retired financier and former presidential advisor), Kenneth Royall, and Sullivan as having "deserted the ship" during the campaign and that they had "basked in the October sunshine on the golf course . . . lifting no finger to help Truman," apparently convinced that "Dewey was going to win."

During the campaign Sullivan was faced with dealing with obviously politically driven but quixotic executive directives issued by Truman. The president demanded the strengthening of the reserve forces, but while acknowledging that the military services had asked for $23 billion for fiscal year 1950, said that they must adhere to the $15 billion cap he had previously set. He then said that the $15 billion limit would be lifted only if "world conditions so indicated." At the same time Truman prohibited public comment on the defense budget by those in the National Military Establishment.

John L. did attend the Democratic convention, which was held in Philadelphia. He became very concerned with the slow pace of the proceedings on the evening of the nomination vote:

> The timetable didn't progress very satisfactorily, and I pleaded with [Howard McGrath, later attorney general and senator from Rhode Island, who was presiding at the convention] to advance the time for Vice President Barkley's talk so that President Truman could get on the air while people were still up and listening to their radios. But Howard ruled otherwise, and I have often wondered how many

people did hear President Truman. It was very early
in the morning.

In fact, until October, Sullivan also doubted whether Truman could
really win the election that year. But then he was given an interesting list by Emil Hurja, who was the statistician for Jim Farley,
now chairman of the Democratic National Committee. That list
showed that there were twelve counties in the country that had
been carried by the successful candidate for the presidency since
1896. Two of those counties were Coos and Strafford in New
Hampshire. The others were Fayette in Pennsylvania, Marion in
West Virginia, Vandenburgh in Indiana, Jasper and Palo in Iowa,
Belmont in Ohio, Albany and Laramie in Wyoming, Crook in
Oregon, and San Joaquin in California. Sullivan visited the two
New Hampshire counties and three of those in the other states
and concluded that "very definitely Truman had a chance and was
coming along fast." Sullivan also felt that Alben Barkley, the vice
presidential candidate, was making a "great contribution" to the
campaign.

On election eve John and Priscilla were home in Manchester where they had gone to vote. No one knew until the next
morning that Truman had won. John admitted that the people in
New Hampshire were surprised by the result. He could smile to
himself that his own comments at Governor Fuller's dinner party
a month earlier, based on his knowledge of the situation in the key
counties on Hurja's list, had been proven true.

While the details of Sullivan's involvement in the 1948
campaign were not documented, he noted in a letter to his mother
on November 8 that he had been to the White House:

> I had a fine conference with the President on Sat-
> urday morning. He sent for me to discuss future
> Naval policy, and to tell me how grateful he was for
> everything I had done for him during the campaign.

10

Dramatic Resignation

Louis A. Johnson was a big two-hundred-fifty-pound hulking man who had no compunctions about pushing people around. Born in 1891 in Roanoke, Virginia, he graduated from the University of Virginia in 1912 with a degree in law. He moved to Clarksburg, West Virginia, where he first served as an assistant prosecuting attorney for Harrison County and then opened a law firm with two other UVA graduates that became known as Steptoe and Johnson. He was elected to the West Virginia House of Delegates in 1916 where he became majority floor leader and chairman of the Judiciary Committee. In World War I he was an officer in charge of an ammunition unit and participated in the Meuse-Argonne offensive, the key battle that led to the end of the war. While awaiting his return to the States, he wrote a sixty-seven-page letter to the Army chief of staff detailing what he perceived to be the Army's inadequacies.

After the war Johnson returned to Clarksburg where he married the wealthy Ruth Maxwell, helped found the American Legion, and concentrated on building his law firm's practice. He involved himself increasingly in Democratic Party politics and from 1932 to 1934 he became national commander of the American Legion, a position that he deftly manipulated to get to know many influential people and spread his reputation throughout the country. Johnson urged the Legionnaires to support the programs of Franklin Roosevelt and invited the newly elected president to speak at the Legion's annual convention in Chicago in 1933.

Immediately following Roosevelt's reelection in 1936, Johnson began lobbying for the post of secretary of war. When the nod for that position went to Harry Woodring, Johnson was bitterly disappointed and initially rejected Jim Farley's urgings that he take the assistant secretary slot. Johnson apparently changed his mind when, according to him, Farley promised that Johnson would shortly be moved up to secretary. During the period when he was assistant secretary, from 1937 to 1940, Johnson became an advocate for the expansion of military aviation, but clashed with Woodring over sending armaments to Great Britain. Johnson made the mistake of publicly criticizing Woodring and bragging that he would soon replace the weak secretary. Even outsiders observed that it was obvious that Johnson was trying "to cut Woodring's throat and get his job."

Sullivan was dragged into the fighting between Woodring and Johnson when:

> President Roosevelt asked Secretary Morgenthau to try to get them together, and since Morgenthau knew I was a friend of both of them, he had me sit in with him in the rather curious role, almost as an interpreter (between the Secretary of War and his own Assistant Secretary!), because the two men wouldn't speak to each other, and I'd ask them the questions and they'd answer me. . . . I think Johnson had charge of industrial development, and I always suspected that he wanted to go ahead faster with rearmament than Secretary Woodring cared to go.

During the same period, Johnson played a prime role in the elevation of George Marshall to be deputy chief of staff, but Marshall was wary of Johnson, concerned that his aggressiveness was having a debilitating effect on the morale of the War Department.

Notwithstanding Johnson's progress in improving procurement practices and advancing military preparedness, when Woodring was asked by Roosevelt to resign in June 1940 after the fall of France to Hitler, the president turned to Henry L. Stimson, a well-known New York lawyer who had earlier been both secretary of war and secretary of state, as Woodring's replacement and Robert Patterson as Stimson's assistant secretary. Johnson was devastated and felt betrayed, but his pleas were rejected by Roosevelt. Even though the president offered him a couple of other posts, Johnson was not mollified and returned to his law practice in Clarksburg. Later during the war he did serve as alien property custodian for the American operations of the German chemical plant I.G. Farben and as the president's personal representative to India.

Within a few months after Truman became president, Steptoe and Johnson opened an office in Washington, D.C., the first step in a long-planned effort by Johnson to escalate his national presence. That step facilitated the next important step in his comeback—in the 1948 presidential campaign he became Truman's main fund-raiser. A revealing anecdote is that in the early morning after the election after he was confident that Truman was the winner, he telephoned Jean Kearney, an assistant for the Democratic National Committee, and told her immediately to type up a list of names of people who had declined to give money during the campaign or who might now be willing to give more and to send a request letter to each of them. "Kearney protested, 'I've been up all night and I think I'm getting pneumonia.' Showing no mercy, Johnson said, 'I didn't ask you how you felt, I told you to do it now.'" There was no doubt that the money he raised proved to be critical to Truman's victory, and Johnson immediately began actively lobbying to be named secretary of defense. When Forrestal resigned on March 28, 1949, Johnson was ready; he was sworn in on the same day.

Johnson's assumption of the office of defense secretary made Sullivan's job significantly more difficult. Truman was becoming convinced that the Air Force and the atom bomb constituted the first line of the country's defense and he was not about to stand in the way of Johnson, in whom he had, at that point, strong confidence as an administrator, to implement that objective. But it was widely recognized that "Johnson viewed the military establishment and the Navy in particular as his personal and deadly enemy" and that he harbored a "really bitter loathing of Naval Aviation and the Marine Corps."

A larger problem was that Johnson was at that point anticipating that Truman might not run again, and Johnson himself and others regarded Johnson as an "unannounced candidate for president." Johnson had already had films made, as Truman had done for himself four years earlier, about and in support of Johnson, to be shown in towns around the country; they were already in the cans and ready to be distributed. When former Secretary of War Harry Woodring heard of the appointment, he said, "There is but one weakness I have observed in him. Louis is over-ambitious in the same way that some men are over-sexed." Driven by his desire, as secretary, Johnson, with Truman's acquiescence, embarked on a campaign to achieve even further Defense Department unification and to drastically reduce defense expenditures, putting him in a position later to run for president on an austerity ticket. He adopted the very political-sounding slogan that the taxpayer was going to get "a dollar's worth of defense for every dollar spent." While the Navy and the Marine Corps were his prime targets, the Army and the Air Force were also pressured to hold costs down. He did not advertise the fact that while Forrestal's office budget in 1949 was $9 million, for 1950, Johnson's first year, it was $150 million. He also testified to Chairman Vinson that he would save $1 billion to $1.5 billion every year, but refused to identify where the savings would be made. The Defense Department roll under Johnson's regime went from just under sixty people to over 20,000.

The extent of the pressure Sullivan was under to meet Johnson's budget targets is reflected by the fact that before Forrestal's resignation, he had told Forrestal that he would lose thirty thousand men, that he would have to inactivate many ships, air squadrons, and naval air stations, and greatly reduce his shipbuilding, modernization, and research programs—i.e., cut to "the minimum active naval power consistent with our national needs."

The substantive budget pressures were exacerbated by the personal difficulties in dealing with Johnson on a day-to-day basis. In that regard, a Navy historian recorded:

> That working with Johnson was difficult was revealed early. Herbert Riley [Forrestal's and then Johnson's naval aide] stated that "he wasn't a man

you could argue with or to whom you could make a logical presentation. Usually he would get up and walk out on you. Or, if he listened he would throw you out of his office when you finished—without a word." . . . When Major General A.W. Vanaman, USAF, commandant of the Industrial College of the Armed Services, began to brief Johnson about the college, Johnson suddenly bellowed: "To Hell with all that. What I want to know is whether you or your officers have any doubts about who is the boss of this establishment?" Vanaman replied: "Well, I don't think so, Sir." Johnson retorted: "You don't *think* so. . . . Well, let me tell you that any one who doesn't cooperate with me won't have his job when the sun comes up in the morning."

On April 4, 1949, the United States and eleven other nations signed the North Atlantic Treaty, in which they pledged their collective security and nonaggression. Immediately Symington and Johnson added another argument to their position—that with the assurance of the availability of NATO land bases, there was less need for naval aviation than ever before.

On April 20, five days after the keel of the new supercarrier *United States* had been laid down at Newport News, Virginia, on April 18, Sullivan talked to Johnson about the ship:

We had laid the keel and I talked to him on a Wednesday afternoon and he asked me if I were to start all over again would I bother to build the ship, and I replied that I most definitely would, that it had been approved by Congress twice and by the President twice, and I saw no reason not to go ahead. I said "Now I'm leaving for Corpus Christi on Friday. I'm addressing a Reserve Officers' convention down there on Saturday, and do I have your word that nothing will be done about this until I have a further opportunity to talk with you?"

He said, "You have my word."

The contract for the construction of the ship had been awarded to Newport News Shipbuilding in August 1948, and the Navy had already spent $6 million on plans, materials, construction of ways, and other preparatory work.

On April 21 Secretary of the Army Kenneth Royall resigned, stating that he had stayed on long enough to assist in the transition.

It was not long before the shoe dropped on the Navy. On April 22 Sullivan testified before the House Appropriations Committee, reiterating that control of the seas was vital to the nation and its defense and that the uninterrupted flow of critical materials from overseas was critical to the livelihood of Americans.

Immediately after his testimony, as he had informed Johnson, Sullivan flew to Corpus Christi, Texas, where on Saturday, April 23, he gave a speech that evening to a Reserve Officers Association conference. While he was there, back in Washington, Johnson sent to Sullivan a two-sentence memorandum, already made public, in which he ordered Sullivan to cancel construction of the supercarrier.

When advised of the Johnson memorandum by telephone after his speech, Sullivan flew back to Washington early the next day. As he watched the piney woods of Texas turn to the green Kentucky hills as the Navy DC-3 droned eastward into the morning sun toward the nation's capital, he must have been enraged at Johnson's mendacity and enormously frustrated that all his budget-juggling efforts and the sacrifices necessary to birth the supercarrier were to be for naught. Rushing to the Pentagon on Sunday afternoon, he learned that Johnson was out of town. He then received a briefing from Chief of Naval Operations Louis Denfield. Sullivan then called Captain Robert L. Dennison, Truman's naval aide, at the White House to come over to his office. Sullivan showed Dennison a draft letter of resignation addressed to the president. Dennison noted that it was "a pretty strong letter" and called Charles Ross, the president's press secretary, who told Sullivan that under no circumstances should he send such a letter to the president and that if he insisted on resigning he should send a letter to Johnson. Sullivan replied that the president, not Johnson, had appointed him. Ross and Dennison then pointed out that Sullivan should not do anything that would damage his personal friendship with Truman. Thereupon Sullivan switched the addressee on the letter to Johnson and wrote a shorter, polite letter to the president. However, on Ross's insistence, he did not send either letter at that point and agreed to meet with Truman first. Three days passed during which the president attempted to get Sullivan to change his mind, but to no avail. Sullivan felt that the manner in which Johnson had acted, including going public with it even before Sullivan was informed, left him no choice:

> "Are you determined to resign?" President Truman asked him via his public relations officer, Charles Ross, when Ross came to Sullivan's office.
>
> "Yes," Sullivan replied. "Johnson is going to abolish the Marine Corps next. I have to make a public stand."
>
> "Very well," Ross replied. "Would you be willing to change your letter of resignation and have it addressed to Secretary of Defense Johnson rather than President Truman?" He added that President Truman didn't want the record to show that he had ever been in disagreement with Sullivan.
>
> Truman knew that Sullivan's letter would be a scorcher, and so it was.

On Tuesday, April 26, Sullivan sent and publicly released the two letters. The first, addressed to Louis Johnson, was as follows:

> My Dear Mr. Secretary:
>
> On Saturday, April 23, without discussion with the Chief of Naval Operations, without consultation with the Secretary of the Navy, you directed the discontinuance of the construction of the USS *United States*, the construction of which had twice been approved by the President.
>
> This carrier had been the subject of intensive study in the Navy Department since it was first proposed early in 1944 by the late Admiral Marc A. Mitscher whose combat experience had convinced him of the necessity.

In a hearing with the Director of the Budget on 15 Dec., 1947, with the approval of the Chief of Naval Operations and the Chief of the Bureau of Ships, I volunteered to surrender $307,000,000 which was the cost to complete the approved construction of other vessels, to insure that funds would be available for the USS *United States*.

Its construction was explicitly approved by the reports of the Armed Services Committees of the Senate and the House on 2 June, 1948, and 9 June, 1948, respectively. In the Naval Appropriation Act for the fiscal year 1949 the appropriation for the first year of construction of the USS *United States* was approved by the Congress.

Again on 17 Dec., 1948, in a conference with the Secretary of Defense and the Director of the Bureau of the Budget, with the approval of the Chief of Naval Operations and the Chief of the Bureau of Ships, I abandoned construction of other vessels in the amount of $57,000,000 to assure the continuance of the carrier and other vessels.

Additional funds for the continuing construction of this vessel in the fiscal year 1950 were included in the budget message which the President sent to the Congress on 3 Jan., 1949, and were included in the National Military Establishment appropriation bill passed by the House on 13 April, 1949.

Professional naval men, charged with the task of planning for a Navy adequate to the defense of America believe that the construction of the USS *United States* is so indispensable to the continuing development of American sea power that they have twice sacrificed other substantial construction because of the carrier's highest naval priority.

On Monday, 18 April, while discussing a variety of subjects with you, the question of the continuance of work on the USS *United States* was raised, and my opinion was asked. I started to give my opinion, but before I had talked more than a minute you advised me that you had another appointment and would discuss this matter with me at a later date.

The following day I sent you a very brief memorandum touching on only one phase of the justification of this carrier. In this memorandum I referred to my desire to resume the discussions that had been interrupted the previous day.

I heard nothing about this again until Saturday, 23 April, while in Corpus Christi, Tex., I was advised by long distance telephone that you had sent me a memorandum directing the discontinuance of construction.

I am, of course, very deeply disturbed by your action, which, so far as I know, represents the first attempt ever made in this country to prevent the development of a powerful weapon. The conviction that this will result in a renewed effort to abolish the Marine Corps and to transfer all naval and marine aviation elsewhere adds to my anxiety.

However, even of greater significance is the unprecedented action on the part of a Secretary of Defense in so drastically and arbitrarily restricting the plans of an armed service without consulting with that service. The consequences of such a procedure are far-reaching and can be tragic.

In view of the foregoing, I am sure you will agree with me that no useful purpose can now be served by my remaining as Secretary of the Navy. I have accordingly submitted my resignation to the President.

I deeply regret the circumstances that lead to my departure from the National Military Establishment at such an interesting and crucial period of its development.

Sincerely,
John L. Sullivan

Sullivan's separate letter of resignation to President Truman read:

> My dear Mr. President:
>
> It is with profound regret that I submit to you my resignation as Secretary of the Navy effective at the earliest date convenient to you.
>
> It is almost four years since you called me back into Federal service. For the three appointments you have conferred upon me and, even more, for the day to day considerations, kindness, and friendliness you have manifested toward me, I shall always be grateful.
>
> I send you my very best wishes for your continued good health and the success of your Administration. More deeply than words can express, I regret the circumstances that prevent me from continuing in my present post to help you in your magnificent efforts.
>
> Very sincerely yours,
> John L. Sullivan

Truman's reply, sent immediately the same day, stated:

> Dear John:
>
> I have read your letter of this day and deeply regret that you feel impelled to relinquish your post.
>
> Greatly as I regret your decision, I have no recourse but to accept, however reluctantly, your resignation as Secretary of the Navy. As to effective date, I desire to meet your personal convenience.
>
> I cannot write this letter without expressing my heartfelt appreciation and our country's appreciation of your valuable service to the nation. You brought to the three posts to which I appointed you high integrity and a wide experience as a man of affairs. You have discharged your various duties with outstanding ability and efficiency.

> Needless to say, you carry with you into private life my best wishes for your continued happiness and success.
>
> Very sincerely yours,
> Harry S. Truman

The story of the resignation blazed across the front pages of the country's newspapers. The full texts of the letters were printed in *The New York Times, The Washington Post,* and many other papers and magazines throughout the nation.

Johnson never responded to Sullivan or even acknowledged Sullivan's points. Rather, he chose to take verbal potshots at Sullivan, such as when he said, "Sullivan has joined the aircraft carrier on personal grounds, and I believe that he . . . will soon regret his action of today." Later Johnson disingenuously tried to say that Sullivan had really resigned a month earlier, denied that he had ever been discourteous to Sullivan, and tried to say that Sullivan needed to go because he was an opponent of unification. Johnson made public three memoranda from the Army (General Omar Bradley), the Navy (Admiral Denfield) and the Air Force (General Hoyt Vandenberg), purporting to reflect a 2-1 "vote" from the Joint Chiefs against the carrier (Bradley's position against the ship was a reversal of the one he had recently espoused.) In point of fact, Johnson did not even receive the three memos until *after* his press release announcing the carrier's cancellation was circulated to reporters. At the time, the Chairman of the Joint Chiefs, General Dwight Eisenhower, was recuperating in Georgia. Ike's position on the carrier had been clearly stated for some time. On December 28, 1948 he wrote to Secretary of Defense Forrestal:

> Personally, I believe that it is wise to continue the building of one supercarrier. I label it, in my mind... as an *interim or emergency weapon*...I do believe it is conceivable that such an instrument could have a very great influence, particularly in the early stages of a war, in dispersing defenses by presenting an instant threat from many different directions and in occasionally driving home a shot that might have real consequences.

He confirmed this position even more strongly in his diary in February, 1949:

> Van[denberg] will not agree Navy needs any carrier larger than [an] escort type. I feel that in the first months of war a few big carriers might be our greatest asset. I want to keep 10 in [the] active fleet—about 6-8 of which should be always in operation.

It appears, therefore, that the military point of view on the carrier was something quite other than uniformly negative. When challenged about his use of the memoranda, Johnson replied, "Whether the Joint Chiefs vote two-to-one or unanimously, they are only advisers to the Secretary of Defense and the President who do the deciding." In fact Johnson had made up his own mind well before April 23. He never claimed to have consulted with Eisenhower on the matter before his announcement. After the dispute became public and Johnson's move a *fait accompli*, Ike understandably could say nothing further on the subject that would conflict with two of his Chiefs' memoranda.

When questioned by a historian, Sullivan confirmed that before he wrote his resignation letter, he had verified with others that Johnson had informally allocated all the Navy and Marine Corps flying personnel and all the aircraft, dividing it between the Navy and the Air Force, and abolishing Marine Corps aviation as a trial balloon for abolishing the Marine Corps itself.

Later in the evening of the day he resigned, Sullivan was at a cocktail party where Secretary of State Dean Acheson shook his hand and said, "Welcome to the most exclusive club in America." "What club is that?" Sullivan queried. "The club of men in public life who have resigned in a cause of conscience," Acheson responded. "Who are the other members of the club?" Sullivan then asked. "Just you and me and Lew Douglas," Acheson said, referring to when he had resigned from the Roosevelt administration in 1933 and Lewis Douglas's resignation as director of the budget in 1934.

In fact, Acheson missed the point entirely: Sullivan had become a member of a truly exclusive "club" to which Acheson did not belong. It was documented in 1975 that of the 389 persons who were presidential appointees and resigned on a point of principle, in the history of our republic only twelve of those, counting Sullivan, have then *also gone public to defend that principle.* That is a rare occurrence in American politics where the usual course is simply for the person to say something to the press such as he or she is resigning "for personal reasons" or "to spend more time with my family." By contrast, in a parliamentary system such as Britain's, it is common for a resigning high appointee to declare that he or she is doing so because of a flawed policy of the prime minister. In their 1975 book, *Resignations in Protest,* Edward Weisband and Thomas Franck concluded:

> There are dramatic, but also dramatically few, instances of persons who openly attack policy. Even more rare is the resigner who points the finger at the Chief Executive or at specific former colleagues. Elliott Richardson, William Ruckelshaus, Webster Davis, William Jennings Bryan, Lindley Garrison, Henry Breckinridge, John Sullivan, James Farley, Henry Wallace, Harold Ickes and Kenneth Davis stand out like lonely stooks of wheat on a flat prairie. That this is so should be of deep concern to those who care about the ethical condition of American government and politics.

On May 3 Sullivan stopped at La Guardia airport and telephoned Nimitz, who was then serving on the United States Military Commission to the United Nations. Nimitz came out to the airport where Sullivan sat in a car with him and told him the details of his resignation and his concerns that Johnson's plans endangered the security of the country.

Sullivan formally left his post on May 24 in a colorful ceremony at the Pentagon described in the *New York Times* the following day:

> A boatsman's mate piped the Secretary "overside" as an honor guard of four platoons of seamen and Marines presented arms. A battery of Marines, up from Quantico, Va., sounded a nineteen-gun salute from their own artillery pieces.

It was a Navy ceremony, but prominent spectators included Louis Johnson, Secretary of Defense; W. Stuart Symington, Secretary of the Air Force; Gordon Gray, Acting Secretary of the Army, and most of the high command of the military forces.

For Secretary Johnson, Mr. Sullivan had a swift, curt handshake. In his letter of resignation a month ago, the Navy Secretary accused the defense chief of arbitrarily halting work on the super aircraft carrier and ignoring him, Mr. Sullivan, in making that decision.

In a brief farewell statement, Mr. Sullivan delivered a "well done" to all Navy and Marine Corps personnel. He urged them to show the incoming Secretary, Francis P. Matthews, "the same loyalty you have to former Secretaries Frank Knox, James Forrestal and myself."

He said he would always be grateful for the chance to serve with his service colleagues "during the war and since, in the greatest Navy the world has ever known, a Navy no foreign foe has ever defeated."

The Marine Corps band played "The Marine's Hymn" and "Anchors Aweigh" while Mr. Sullivan inspected the honor guard with Admiral Lewis E. Denfield, Chief of Naval Operations and General Clifton B. Cates, commandant of the Marine Corps.

The formality was lightened somewhat at the end by the band's breaking into "When Irish Eyes Are Smiling" and finally, "Auld Lang Syne" as Mr. Sullivan and his family drove off.

Louis Johnson's biographers described how it was that Johnson came to be at the going-away ceremony:

Sullivan's resignation immediately became a cause célèbre for navy brass. He was hailed as a man of principle who was willing to sacrifice his career for a just and noble purpose. While the admirals were holding a quiet farewell ceremony for Sullivan on the day he was to leave the Pentagon, Johnson seized the arm of one of his senior aides, Brigadier General Louis Renfrow, and said, "Come on, we're going over there." Renfrow was shocked. "Mr. Secretary, you can't do that. When Al Capone kills them in Chicago, he sends them flowers, but he doesn't go to their funeral." Johnson replied, "John [Sullivan] and I are good friends. We're both members out at Burning Tree. He understands." With Renfrow in tow, Johnson barged into the ceremony. Said Renfrow later, "These admirals, they looked daggers at him."

The media and public reaction following Sullivan's leaving was mixed. Outcry against Johnson's high-handed act was balanced by the feeling that Navy ships would have to give way to Air Force planes and the atom bomb that they could deliver.

President Truman later told White House aide Eben Ayers that he "did not greatly blame Sullivan" for what he had done.

Sullivan's resignation in protest of the cancellation of the supercarrier triggered what became known as the "Revolt of the Admirals." Johnson's continuous reduction of other Navy ships and equipment needed for conventional force readiness further fueled the revolt. Due to the lack of operating funds, ships were mothballed and the Navy and the Marine Corps were deprived of their preeminent amphibious capability.

In congressional hearings before Carl Vinson's House Armed Services Committee and in other public arenas, the Navy reacted angrily to Johnson's actions. Admirals Denfield, Radford, and Gallery and Captains Arleigh "Thirty-one Knot" Burke and Fitzhugh Lee led the assault for the Navy, and the Marine Corps leaders were Generals Alexander Archer Vandegrift (commandant), Clifton Cates (his successor), and Holland Smith, and Lieutenant General Oliver Prince. The Navy focused on what they perceived to be the deficiencies of the B-36 bomber, principally that it had limited range and was vulnerable to Soviet jet interceptors. The Air Force fought back with data supporting the B-36 and minimizing the effectiveness of naval surface ships in future major wars. The Air Force arguments were based on the atom bomb being the sole and ultimate solution to the nation's security.

Typical of the bitterness that emerged among the admirals about the new secretary of the Navy's views attempting to support Johnson was a letter written by Vice Admiral Gerald F. Bogan, commander of the First Task Fleet in the Pacific, to Matthews, but leaked to the press:

> The creation of three departments or sub departments where formerly there were but two is not unification. Under the present law it can be made to and does operate effectively in the field. But it would be sheer balderdash to assume that there has been anything approaching it [unification] among the Secretariat, the Joint Staff, or the high command of all three services. . . .
>
> The morale of the navy is lower today than at any time since I entered the commissioned ranks in 1916 . . . [and] in my opinion, this descent, almost to despondency, stems from complete confusion as to the future role of the Navy and its advantages or disadvantages as a permanent career. . . . We . . . are fearful that the country is being . . . sold a bill of goods.

Bogan's letter gave rise to a mad scrambling within the Navy between those who agreed strongly with it and those who also did but sided with Matthews to preserve their careers.

The arguments dragged on endlessly, ultimately resulting in the firing of Chief of Naval Operations Denfield by Sullivan's successor, Francis Matthews, and Johnson, and the naming of Admiral Forrest Sherman as Denfield's replacement.

John Sullivan's successor as secretary of the Navy, Francis P. Matthews, was a Roman Catholic banker, corporate executive, and attorney from Omaha, Nebraska, whom the press labeled "the rowboat secretary" because that was the only kind of boat he had ever sailed. Sullivan's comment was, "I have been told that Secretary Johnson phoned around to his old American Legion friends and specifically requested that they recommend a prominent Catholic to take my place. The inference of that, of course, was that he was planning to run for president and he didn't want to offend the Catholic voters."

* * *

At six o'clock in the morning of August 29, 1949, in Central Asia north of the city of Semipalatinsk, the Soviet Union exploded a nuclear device similar to the bomb dropped on Nagasaki, Japan by the United States in 1945. The event triggered a new, more dramatic international arms race that would emphasize the usefulness and importance of aircraft carriers in American foreign policy.

The Navy never abandoned its quest for a new large-deck aircraft carrier, and the design process accelerated when the Korean War broke out in 1950. Secretary of Defense Johnson reversed field and promised the Navy it could have another carrier as soon as it wanted one. The doctrine of massive nuclear retaliation gave way to a more flexible-response approach in which carriers again became a major factor. The result was the USS *Forrestal*, CV-59, launched at Newport News Shipbuilding and Dry Dock Company in Newport News, Virginia, on December 11, 1954, and commissioned on October 1, 1955. There followed three more *Forrestal*-class ships and four other conventionally powered carriers until the world's first nuclear-powered aircraft carrier, the USS *Enterprise*, was delivered on November 25, 1961. Next came the USS *Nimitz*, delivered on May 3, 1975, and nine more *Nimitz*-class ships. The to-be USS *Gerald R. Ford*, the first of a new class of nuclear-powered aircraft carriers, is currently under construction at the Huntington Ingalls Industries shipyard in Virginia. It is estimated for delivery to the Navy in 2015. Over fifty years of new aircraft carrier construction have passed since the keel of the USS *Forrestal* was laid.

These vessels are now dubbed by the Navy as "four and a half acres of U.S. territory" that are mobile, and the United States does not have to rely on permission from foreign governments to store and launch its aircraft. It is well documented that when the United States is faced with imminent war, the president's first question is often, "Where are the aircraft carriers?" Even in the second decade of the twenty-first century, carriers continue to play an important and expanding role. Carrier-based aircraft provided cover when the United States went into Afghanistan after 9/11. Navy planes made 75 percent of all strike sorties, flying off four carriers. When Turkey and Saudi Arabia refused American requests to operate Air Force jets from land bases in support of Operation Iraqi Freedom in 2003, more than half of all American sorties were flown by Navy carrier-based pilots. These vessels are also now launching nonpiloted drones. Carriers are playing significant roles in providing disaster relief and humanitarian aid: the USS *Abraham Lincoln* led relief efforts during the 2004 Asian tsunami. Also reflecting the present-day importance of aircraft carriers is the fact that the Chinese Navy is now focusing its efforts on them.

Similarly, Sullivan's support of the Marines has proven to be justified. This "ready-to-go" force has been the one to go into harm's way first in many crises in recent years. Since 1949 the Marine Corps has continued to demonstrate its prowess as the country's only amphibious force—on the Pusan Peninsula in Korea in 1950 and then again at the landing at Inchon, then in 1958 in Lebanon, and as well at Da Nang, Vietnam, in 1965 and Kuwait in 1991. It has also been a key participant both in Iraq (including cleaning insurgents out of Fallujah and then Ramadi) and in Afghanistan continuing through 2011. All the while it has continued to add to its capabilities in new areas including counterinsurgency, counterterrorism, intelligence gathering, cyber espionage, and cyber warfare. The Corps has demonstrated time and again that it can significantly supplement the Army's capabilities without engaging in unneeded, expensive duplication. Its esprit de corps is unmatched anywhere else in the nation's military.

When the Democrats came back into power in 1960, Sullivan was not considered for a position in the John F. Kennedy administration, but that did not matter to him at that point; his good judgment had long since been strongly vindicated.

Two historians have commended Sullivan for the way in which he conducted himself following his resignation:

After [his] mercurial blast . . . Sullivan went back to his law firm and did not speak on the issue in public again. "I was swamped with invitations to lecture," he has said, "but I refused them all. I had made my point. Anything more would have seemed like carping. However, resigning did give me the opportunity to work quietly behind the scenes with the key Members of Congress. I knew them all, you know, their families and histories. That happens after a while, when you work your way up from an Assistant Secretaryship. And we did get the carrier eventually."

The historians' comment points to the irony in the fact that Sullivan, who much preferred in both his public and private careers to work effectively behind the scenes, was forced to take the most significant step in his life by resorting to laying down a gauntlet in the full public glare.

As to Johnson personally, Sullivan confined himself to the diplomatic comment that in the handling of the position of secretary of defense, Johnson had "centralized [the department] too much, and expanded it too far and too fast." It was Louis Johnson's own dogged adherence to a defense policy that relied almost solely on the atom bomb and the Air Force's B-36 strategic bombers that eventually did him in. The Korean War exposed the error of Johnson's ill-conceived budget cutbacks in conventional force readiness. The consequent public criticism led President Truman to ask for Johnson's resignation on September 19, 1950, and to replace him with General George Marshall. Johnson's own former aide, Vice Admiral Herbert D. Riley, summed up the opinion of many observers:

[Johnson's political ambition] was evident in his many speeches, his publicity machine and most of all in his deliberate slashing of our Presidentially-approved and Congress-approved military programs, in the belief that if he slashed approved military programs under the guise of "cutting fat—not muscle," he could curry public favor—and votes. He wanted the SecDef job simply because the Defense Department budget was the largest opportunity to "save the taxpayers" mammoth sums and thereby form his election platform. Korea crossed him up—and forever out of the government, thank God.

Riley's judgment was confirmed by the award-winning author William Manchester, who wrote: "Johnson was Truman's son-of-a-bitch, a rumpled, bumbling Democratic Joe Martin who Acheson thought was afflicted with 'a brain malady.'"

John Sullivan was the last in the line of Navy secretaries with official significant power at the top level of the government. During World War II and previously, there was no Department of Defense, only the Navy Department and the War Department (which was the Department of the Army prior to the war). The secretaries of both those two departments were members of the president's Cabinet. Forrestal was the last Navy secretary who enjoyed full Cabinet status. Sullivan, Forrestal's successor, assumed the post after the passage of the National Security Act; hence he did not have Cabinet status, but he was still a member of the National Security Council, affording him direct access to Truman on national security issues. (During his time as secretary, he met with President Truman "two or three times a week, sometimes only once a month.") The 1949 amendments to the National Security Act, effective after Sullivan had left, downgraded the Navy secretary still further, removing membership on the National Security Council.

PART III

Life on the Outside Again

11

Respected, Behind the Scenes

After his resignation Sullivan once again settled into the practice of law. He rejoined Lawrence Bernard and Jack Shea in the firm of Sullivan, Bernard and Shea that he had formed in April, 1945, and from which he had been on a leave of absence while he was at Navy. They had offices in the new Ring Building at the corner of 18th and M streets in the northwest sector of Washington. In November, 1950, W. John Kenney, who had been Sullivan's undersecretary at the Navy Department, became a name partner. They also had as associates George McMurray, a tax law expert, and later in 1950, Henry Beauregard, a government contracts specialist who had been Sullivan's special assistant at the Navy Department. (The firm's name ultimately became Sullivan and Beauregard.) Sullivan never grew the firm significantly, preferring to keep it small and intimate with just two or three substantive specialties rather than enlarging it to compete with the city's big all-purpose firms such as Covington and Burling. The small size also suited and facilitated his personal style in handling cases, which was to quietly provide advice and assistance behind the scenes, with the general public most often being completely unaware of his involvement.

The firm was a most pleasant place to practice law. Sullivan's personal views about the proper way to run a law firm and conduct business guided the manner in which the firm's attorneys viewed business and the federal government and practiced their profession. Sullivan's guidelines and observations included:

Regarding general work philosophy: "If there's work to be done, we work around the clock until it is completed; after that everyone should get out of the office for a break."

He often referred to the firm basically as a "club" of compatible lawyers. He always insisted that each new lawyer be able to "get along" with every one of the others.

"You can only tell a client that he's crazy a limited number of times."

"I never made a good deal in a hurry." Said when under pressure to make an unfavorable deal; this was from a man who made many good deals in a hurry when he wanted to.

"In Washington, very often a bad decision on Monday is better than a good decision on Friday."

"During the first six months of any new Administration there are a lot of surprises. Some of the appointments which everyone perceives as being very good do not pan out. Others seen as weak turn out to be excellent."

"There is a great psychological difference between the authority to recommend and the power to decide. Hence, many a good Under Secretary has flopped when promoted to be Secretary of a Department."

"In Washington it's best and most satisfying, when handling a matter successfully for a client, that no one on the outside ever knows you were involved."

Sullivan always took a close personal interest in the health and welfare of each attorney in the firm and in their families. Whenever someone was ill, he was sure to receive a telephone call from John L. asking after his well-being and urging him to recover fully before trying to return to work.

Notwithstanding the firm's small size, it immediately attracted a sizable stable of blue-chip clients, including Martin

Marietta, Newport News Shipbuilding, Magnavox, N.V. Philips, Southern Pacific Railroad, General Tire and Rubber Company, National Lead Company, Hazeltine Corporation, United States Lines, Grumman Corporation, Braniff Airways, General Electric, Boston and Maine Railroad, Citibank, Bunker Ramo Corporation, and Sweden's Axel Johnson.

The story of how Newport News Shipbuilding became a client of the firm is illustrative of the way in which Sullivan wielded his personality to build the firm's client base. John and Priscilla attended partner Henry Beauregard's wedding in Dublin, Ireland, on September 20, 1952. After the wedding, they returned to the United States aboard the SS *United States*. Within a few minutes after boarding the liner at Cork, John L. received a telephone call in his stateroom from General John Franklin, then president of United States Lines. General Franklin asked John whether he played bridge. Upon receiving an affirmative reply, the general asked Sullivan to join him and some others in his stateroom in ten minutes. Whereupon Sullivan proceeded to spend a substantial portion of the trip home playing bridge with a group of ten to twelve men who kept two tables active throughout the trip. In the evening they would join their wives for dinner and some dancing.

The Sullivans became quite friendly on the trip with General Franklin and his wife, Emily. During the course of their conversations John L. disclosed his interest in hunting and also told Mrs. Franklin that he was particularly fond of hunting and eating grouse.

One evening as they sat down for dinner, the steward announced that they were particularly fortunate that evening to have some very fine-looking grouse on the menu. Mrs. Franklin immediately ordered one for herself and declared that John L. should have one, too. Whereupon John thanked Mrs. Franklin, acknowledged that he indeed enjoyed grouse, but that he thought he would not have one that evening. John placed an order for haddock, and the steward went on around the table. Mrs. Franklin, however, persisted and pressed John once again to order the grouse. John thanked her once again and once again respectfully declined. Somewhat confused and not to be put off, Mrs. Franklin exclaimed, "Give me one good reason why you are not ordering this very fine grouse!" John then explained that he was a Roman Catholic and this was Friday. The erudite Mrs. Franklin pushed him still further, insisting that since Sullivan was traveling he was entitled to a dispensation from fish that evening. John then explained further that he had never paid much attention to the dispensations that the church permitted and that he chose simply to avoid meat altogether on Friday. Mrs. Franklin at that point gave up and allowed John L. to enjoy his haddock.

Afterward, on their way to the card room for another hour or so of bridge, General Franklin drew Sullivan aside and professed his admiration for the manner in which John had politely but firmly stood his ground with Emily. The General explained that he admired a man who was a Democrat, a Catholic, or whatever for all purposes and immediately jumped into the subject of whether Sullivan's firm would be interested in representing United States Lines.

General Franklin's enthusiasm for Sullivan's integrity continued upon their landing in New York. Upon talking to William Blewett, then president of Newport News Shipbuilding and Dry Dock Company, which had built the SS *United States*, Franklin suggested to Blewett that Newport News should also retain Sullivan's firm. Subsequently Blewett and Sullivan became fast friends and mutual admirers wholly independent from Franklin. Sullivan enjoyed many hunting trips with Blewett and others in New Jersey. Newport News Shipbuilding proceeded to grow into a significant client of the firm.

Sullivan's relationship with President Truman continued on a very cordial basis. He later told the following story:

> When I left the Navy, I was importuned to take on all kinds of assignments, and while talking with the President a few weeks after I had left the Navy, I told him that I was being urged to accept the national chairmanship of the National Conference for Christians and Jews, whereon President Truman immediately urged me to accept the appointment, stressing the fact that this organization had never had a Catholic president. In fact, he pressed me so

hard that I finally made a deal with him that if I took it he would address the opening dinner, which I was to move from New York to Washington to take advantage of the greater publicity the organization would get here in Washington than it ever got in the New York newspapers.

He agreed to, and when I moved the dinner from New York to Washington November 11, 1949, he accepted, and brought with him Mrs. Truman, most of the Cabinet, and the majority of the Supreme Court.

Sullivan was also sought after by a number of prestigious corporations to serve on their boards of directors. Among those he agreed to serve on for long periods before he retired were Martin Marietta, Metro-Goldwyn-Mayer, the Brown Paper Company, Aluminium Limited of Canada, and Washington's National Savings and Trust. He was also a director of the Navy League of the United States, a trustee of the Naval Historical Society and the Daniel Webster Council of the Boy Scouts of America, and a member of the board of governors of the United Service Organizations.

Sullivan was always a popular attendee at board meetings, where other members enjoyed his humor and "stories." One story he liked to tell occurred while he was traveling to attend a board meeting of the Brown Paper Company in Berlin, New Hampshire. He rode there by train, accompanied by fellow board member Gene Tunney, the former heavyweight boxing champion who later lectured on Shakespeare at Yale and was a commander in the Navy during World War II. They arrived late at night in the middle of a snowstorm, and the only place available for them to stay was a rather ramshackle hotel on the outskirts of town. When Tunney signed his name first in big, strong letters on the register, the clerk sniffed and said, "Oh, sure. Expect me to believe that you are really Gene Tunney? Where are your medals?" Tunney laughed and said, "You think I've got an unusual name? Wait 'til you hear the next guy!"

In 1951 Sullivan was asked to succeed William Doyle as chairman of the Democratic National Committee. He declined, citing potential conflicts of interest with the firm's clients.

As the year 1952 opened, President Truman appeared to have decided not to be a candidate in the coming November election. He had approached both Chief Justice Fred Vinson and General Eisenhower about leading the Democratic ticket, but both had declined. In January he approached Adlai Stevenson about taking the job, and Stevenson also rejected his appeal. For a period it looked as though the president might reconsider running again. Sullivan spoke to him in an effort to get him to run:

> I thought that it was very important that he remain President for another four years, and I saw no other Democrat who could be elected at that time. He never told me that he was going to become a candidate, and he never told me he was *not* going to become a candidate. I felt it was very important in the New Hampshire primary, the first to be held in the country, that his name be on the ballot.

Sullivan proceeded with Truman's silent acquiescence to take the necessary steps to have Truman's name placed on the ballot in New Hampshire, but Truman refused to announce that he was a candidate, and he did not campaign in the New Hampshire primary. During the primary period, furthermore, Truman made two unfortunate comments—that he considered primaries a lot of "eyewash" and that they were nothing more than "popularity contests." Sullivan raised some money from his Democratic friends in Washington and made three speeches on Truman's behalf in New Hampshire. By contrast, Estes Kefauver from Tennessee and his attractive wife raised a much larger money chest and campaigned hard in the state. Consequently, on March 11 Kefauver won a surprise victory in that primary. Truman's aides were irked by the results, but the president never criticized the efforts of his New Hampshire supporters. The president's other advisers then advised against his running, and in a speech at the Jefferson Jackson Dinner in the National Armory on March 29 he formally announced that he would not run for reelection. Truman's *Memoirs* provide an interesting insight into his thought processes that led him to his decision:

> My decision not to be a candidate for re-election in 1952 goes back to the day of my inauguration in 1949. . . . I found myself thinking about my own future, and how long a man ought to stay in the presidency, and a nation's need for constant renewal of leadership. I now was certain that I would not run again. But I could not share this decision with anyone. By the very nature of his office, this is one secret a President must keep to himself to the last possible moment.
>
> More than a year later, on April 16, 1950, I wrote out my thoughts and my intention in a memorandum which I locked away:
>
> "I am not a candidate for nomination by the Democratic Convention.
>
> "In my opinion eight years as President is enough and sometimes too much for any man to serve in that capacity.
>
> "There is a lure in power. It can get into a man's blood just as gambling and lust for money have been known to do.
>
> "This is a Republic. The greatest in the history of the world. I want the country to continue that way. When Rome forgot Cincinnatus, its downfall began. When we forget the examples of such men as Washington, Jefferson and Andrew Jackson, all of whom could have had a continuation in the office, then will we start down the road to dictatorship and ruin. I know I could be elected again and continue to break the old precedent as it was broken by F.D.R. It should not be done. That precedent should continue not by a Constitutional amendment, but by custom based on the honor of the man in the office.

"Therefore, to re-establish that custom, although by a quibble I could say that I've only had one term, I am not a candidate and will not accept the nomination for another term."

In March of the same year, 1951, I took the memorandum out at the Little White House in Key West and read it to my White House staff. The reaction was to be expected. The staff responded with deep emotion and expressions of protest and disappointment. They pleaded with me not to make public any announcement. But I had no intention of doing this until the proper time.

After the 1946 midterm elections, when the Republicans gained control of both houses of Congress, they sought to prevent a reoccurrence of what Roosevelt had done and proposed a constitutional amendment on May 24, 1947, to limit a president to two terms. But at the time of Truman's memorandum it had not yet been ratified by a sufficient number of states. It was subsequently ratified on February 27, 1951, as the Twenty-second Amendment to the Constitution.

While the campaign slogged on during the next few months, Truman was greatly distressed that no leader in whom he had confidence came forward to lead the party, but the president's attention and efforts during that period were completely consumed with his effort to take over the country's steel mills in order to resolve a wage impasse between the companies and their workers. In the end the Supreme Court thwarted the president's move, but a settlement was reached on July 24, and Truman headed to the Democratic convention already in progress in Chicago. There Kefauver led in delegates, followed by Richard Russell, Averill Harriman, and Adlai Stevenson. A surge arose for Alben Barkley, but that soon subsided with the realization that he was too old. Finally, on the third ballot, a reluctant Stevenson was voted to be the party's standard-bearer.

Sullivan attended the convention, eventually supporting Stevenson, but he remained doubtful that any candidate other than Truman could win. He said:

> I worked very hard for Mr. Stevenson. He had been an assistant to Secretary Knox, and I had known him in that capacity. Until about half way through the campaign, I thought he had a chance, but in the latter half of that campaign, he demonstrated an indecisiveness, which is one of the worst attributes a President can have, and my ardor for him cooled, and I did not vote for his election four years later when he was again nominated.

In the end Sullivan's evaluation was proved right. So was Truman.

The 1952 race was the last one that Sullivan was involved in to any significant degree. In 1976 he was a backer of Senator Henry J. Jackson's early bid, but that faltered early.

Sullivan continued to be an advocate for New Hampshire's interests in Washington. He worked closely with his old adversary, Republican Senator Styles Bridges, on many occasions to convince those on the Democrat side of the aisle to vote for such things as continuing to fund and keep open the state's Portsmouth Naval Shipyard.

He remained an active sportsman for many years, principally as a fisherman and a golfer. At least once a year he traveled to a fishing club on the Ste-Marguerite River in Québec for a week of salmon fishing. Throughout the year, except when he was in New Hampshire during the summer months, he was regularly on the first tee at the Burning Tree Club in Bethesda, Maryland, invariably followed by a gin rummy game after the round. He was a prime mover in the club, serving as its president from 1950 to 1954.

On one occasion President Eisenhower, also an avid golfer and a member of Burning Tree Club, summoned Sullivan to the Oval Office. Expecting the subject to be a serious national issue, John L. promptly hustled over to the White House. When he got there Ike closed the door and explained to John that he would like to have his Protestant minister admitted to membership in Burning Tree and would like Sullivan's help. Without missing a beat, John replied, "Certainly, Mr. President, I'll see that it gets done. Oh, by the way, would you be willing to write a letter of recommendation for my Catholic priest?" Ike laughed and agreed.

Another Burning Tree story is that whenever Sullivan arrived at the long luncheon table for a golf game, he was beset by requests for bets from the others around the table. When the subject of how many handicap strokes he would give each one, he would always say, "Whatever your conscience will allow." One day before Sullivan arrived, the others in the luncheon crowd devised a ruse to fool him: each proceeded to claim an obviously too-large number of strokes and bested Sullivan on all their bets. Always appreciative of a good joke, John L. laughed the hardest when the scores were submitted, and he paid off every bet.

Sullivan was the quintessential "club man" who reveled in the company of other like-minded friends. In addition to Burning Tree, he belonged to the Chevy Chase Club, the Metropolitan Club, the Anglers' Club and The Brook in New York City, and similar Washington organizations, including the Alfalfa, the Friendly Sons of St. Patrick, and the Military Order of the Carabao. In 1957 he was the Alfalfa Club's mock nominee for president of the United States.

He continued for many years to be a popular and sought-after speaker at both government and social occasions.

* * *

Ironically, in his private life Sullivan became involved one final time in a battle where Louis Johnson was on the other side.

In the 1940s Loews Incorporated had become a billion-dollar-plus industrial empire that, among other operations, produced motion pictures under the trade name of Metro-Goldwyn-Mayer. Louis Mayer was the storied "king" of the MGM studio and the prime mover in all of Hollywood. But when MGM lost substantial amounts of money at the end of the decade, Nicholas Schenck, the president of Loews located in New York City, ousted Mayer. When Schenck himself later stepped down in 1956, Mayer saw his chance to return to power, and in the spring of 1957 he mounted a proxy fight to oust management in which he proposed a new slate of directors that included Louis Johnson. John Sullivan was already a director supporting the existing management. The differences in the personalities and style of the two men were further revealed during the protracted legal entanglement that ensued. Johnson charged in, attempting to control the legal strategy of the insurgents, while Sullivan quietly advised in the background as the famed trial lawyer Louis Nizer carefully orchestrated the incumbent management's plan and defensive tactics.

Johnson's aggressiveness and a couple of questionable moves on the challengers' part ultimately enabled Nizer and the new Loews' president, Joseph Vogel, to prevail on October 15, 1957. Johnson was out, and Sullivan was still in as a director. This time Johnson was the loser.

* * *

Sullivan continued to maintain his law partnership in Manchester, New Hampshire, with Edward Wynot. In the late 1950s and early 1960s he was involved in a major dispute for Peter Fuller's Cadillac distributorship at 808 Commonwealth Avenue in Boston, Massachusetts. General Motors had embarked on a campaign to eliminate its distributorships, which covered wide regions and were in effect middlemen between the auto giant and its dealers in the country's cities and towns. The Fuller distributorship covered a significant portion of New England in Massachusetts, New Hampshire, Maine, and Vermont. Based on their own lawyers' advice, the other distributorships around the country were capitulating to GM because of a problematic clause in all their agreements. Against the advice of his father and brother, Peter Fuller determined to fight GM and requested arbitration. He and Sullivan made a presentation to the arbitrator, a Judge Coleman from Baltimore, who rejected GM's arguments. His ruling perpetuated the Fuller contract for an additional five years, a decision that saved the Fuller operation from serious financial difficulties.

In the following years, Sullivan gradually became less active in his New Hampshire law practice. He and Priscilla spent some days at their home in Manchester, but they spent the bulk of their time in New Hampshire at Little Boars Head and Rye Beach, where John played golf at the Abenaqui Golf Club while the family enjoyed their home high above the Atlantic at Little Boars Head.

Sullivan was a member of the Dartmouth College Alumni Council for three years and its president from 1950 to 1951. He then served as a trustee of the college from 1957 until 1968, chairing the board's budget committee for several years. While a trustee he initially opposed coeducation at the college, but later acquiesced to it. He also strongly supported the presence and role of ROTC on the campus. Over the years he made substantial contributions to the college, including the Hopkins Center. He also established the John L. Sullivan Scholarship Fund at Manchester Central High School. Dartmouth, the University of New Hampshire, Loyola University in Baltimore, Duquesne University, and the University of Portland, Oregon, all awarded him honorary doctorate of law degrees.

He continued to be held in high esteem within the state's Democratic Party. When the Republican Senator Charles Tobey died in 1953, Sullivan was pressed to run for the seat, but he quickly squelched the efforts to nominate him.

After a while the bulk of his time was spent playing golf and gin rummy and socializing at his clubs. He died of a heart attack at the Exeter, New Hampshire, hospital on August 8, 1982. A Mass of Christian Burial was celebrated in St. Catherine of Siena Church in Manchester on August 11, and he was buried with full military honors at Arlington Cemetery in Virginia on August 13. As fate would have it, shortly before John L.'s death, a large oak tree at the cemetery reached its last days and had to be cut down. That event made room for a new gravesite opposite that of James Forrestal. There John L. was laid to rest forever, near the man he so admired.

Soon after John's death, it became evident that Priscilla was suffering from Alzheimer's disease. She passed away on January 25, 1994, and was buried in Pine Grove Cemetery in Manchester.

* * *

In 1947 a *Washington Times-Herald* columnist wrote a story about the new secretary of the Navy in which he said:

> Contrary to widespread belief, John L. Sullivan was not named after the "Boston strong boy," although the old bare knuckle fighter has played a big part

in his life. "I wish," said Mr. Sullivan, "that I had a nickel for every poke in the nose I have had to take because of John L. All through my boyhood and even later when I was at Dartmouth and finally Harvard Law School, some Lou was always coming up and sneering: 'So you're John L. Sullivan, eh? All right—put 'em up.'"

John Sullivan did "put 'em up"—for America. His contributions to the nation during World War II and its aftermath were significant and lasting. Equally important is that he demonstrated that in life, guts, integrity, and style count. This man, one more "grandson of Ireland," had all three.

Afterword

*I*n mid-December 1968 I stood up from a hearty lunch at the Madison Hotel in Washington, D.C., and shook hands with my hosts, John L. Sullivan and his law partner, John Kenney. John L. looked me straight in the eye as he pressed my hand and said, "Well, Steve, I am delighted that you will be joining our firm, but I must say that I hope you remember the law better than you do your blankets." I was completely taken aback. What in the world was the man talking about? He proceeded to explain.

Over thirteen years earlier, on the Friday after Labor Day in 1955, I was working as an assistant in the golf pro shop at Abenaqui Golf Club in Rye Beach, New Hampshire. It was a quiet day, as most of the summer residents had headed back earlier in the week to their winter homes in places such as Boston, New York, Philadelphia, and St. Louis. No one was on the course.

At about nine-thirty a.m., two men appeared in the door of the shop. The first was Sullivan, a member whom I knew well, having caddied for him several times before moving up into the shop. The second was his guest, Gene Tunney, the former world heavyweight boxing champion. They reminded me of the cartoon characters Mutt and Jeff: Sullivan was no more than five feet eight inches tall, while Tunney was over six feet.

Sullivan said, "Steve, we need a caddie." I replied, "I'm sorry, Mr. Sullivan, all the caddies went back to school this week; I have none." He eyed me critically and said, "Well, why don't you close up the shop and come out and caddie for us." It was not really a question. His suggestion would leave the shop unattended, but I did a quick mental risk-reward analysis and replied, "Okay, I'll be right with you."

As we made our way down the first fairway, Sullivan asked me, "How about you? What are you doing this fall? Still in school?" I answered that the very next morning I was heading down to New Haven to begin my freshman year at Yale. Nothing more was said on the subject, and we finished the round without incident.

Unbeknownst to me, on the next day, Saturday morning, when I was long gone on the road south, my younger brother, Sandy, having no high school classes or obligations that day, went over to the golf course to caddie. By coincidence he was assigned to caddie for the same two golfers, Sullivan and Tunney. As they prepared to tee off, Sullivan asked my brother, "Did Steve get off okay to New Haven?" My brother replied, "Yes, but he forgot his blankets!"

Until Sullivan braced me with his statement many years later I never knew the second half of the story involving my brother. When Sullivan told me of it, I broke up in laughter at my own mistake and marveled once again at Sullivan's renowned memory for names, incidents, and details of people he had not seen for ages, testimony to an impressive political skill.

I wish that I had his memory, for in truth I should have written this book about him thirty years ago. He and his contemporaries are long gone, and other than a precious few tales, I don't have available answers to many questions that I would have asked him and others. The remaining written record, sparse in some periods, has been my only main resource. I hope that shortcoming does not detract materially from my readers' enjoyment in learning about the interesting career of a remarkable American patriot.

When I began this project I asked Sullivan's daughter Pat to summarize her principal memory of her father. She threw back her head, laughed, and said, "He was a raconteur and a card shark." She was right. John L. was both. But he had many significant accomplishments.

Rye Beach, New Hampshire
September 2011

Bibliography

AUTHOR'S DISCUSSIONS AND INTERVIEWS

John L. Sullivan * Patricia Sullivan Meyers * Charles Sullivan * Deborah Sullivan DuSault * Admiral Robert Carney * Henry G. Beauregard * Mary Manning Cleveland * Lawrence Connell * James County * Philip Drake * Connie Fields * Peter Fuller * Margot Harrington * Pliny Holt * Mary Jo (Mrs. Brendan) Leahey * Lucille Lowry * Tedson Meyers * Bert Whittemore

UNPUBLISHED SOURCES

Manuscript Collections Consulted at the Harry S. Truman Library, Independence, Missouri

Papers of Harry S. Truman
Papers of John L. Sullivan
Papers of W. John Kenney
Papers of Clark Clifford
Papers of Admiral Robert L. Dennison
Papers of Thomas Lynch
Papers of Edward Foley
Papers of Abijah U. Fox

Oral History Transcripts

John L. Sullivan * W. John Kenney * Robert L. Dennison

Manuscript Collections Consulted at the Franklin D. Roosevelt Presidential Library, Hyde Park, New York

President Roosevelt's Personal File

Papers of Henry Morgenthau, Jr.
Papers of Isador Lubin
Papers of Oscar Cox
FDR Memorial Foundation Records
FDR Library Vertical (reference) File
Manuscript Collection Consulted At Dartmouth College's Rauner Special Collections Library, Hanover, New Hampshire
Papers of John L. Sullivan, 1954–1975

BOOKS

Acheson, Dean. *Present at the Creation: My Years in the State Department.* New York: Norton, 1969.

Adams, Henry H. *Harry Hopkins: A Biography.* New York: Putnam, 1977.

Albion, Robert, and Robert Connery. *Forrestal and the Navy.* New York: Columbia University Press, 1962.

Beasley, Norman. *Frank Knox, American: A Short Biography.* Garden City, New York: Doubleday, Doran, 1936.

Blood, Grace Holbrook. *Manchester on the Merrimack: The Story of a City.* Manchester, New Hampshire: L. A. Cummings, 1948.

Blum, John Morton. *From the Morgenthau Diaries.* Vol. 2, *Years of Urgency, 1938-1941.*Boston: Houghton Mifflin, 1965.

Blum, John Morton. *From The Morgenthau Diaries.* Vol. 3, *Years of War, 1941–1945.* Boston: Houghton Mifflin, 1967.

Brands, H. W. *Traitor to His Class: The Privileged Life and Radical Presidency of Franklin Delano Roosevelt.* New York: Doubleday, 2008.

Caraley, Demetrios. *The Politics of Military Unification: A Study of Conflict and the Policy Process.* New York: Columbia University Press, 1966.

Coletta, Paolo E., ed. *American Secretaries of the Navy.* Vol. 2, *1913–1972.* Annapolis: Naval Institute Press, 1980.

Coletta, Paolo E. *The United States Navy and Defense Unification, 1947–1953.* Newark: University of Delaware Press, 1981.

Farley, James A. *Jim Farley's Story: The Roosevelt Years.* New York: Whittlesey House/McGraw-Hill, 1948.

Gabler, Neal. *Walt Disney: The Triumph of the American Imagination.* New York: Knopf, 2006.

Hareven, Tamara, and Randolph Langenbach. *Amoskeag: Life and Work in an American Factory-City.* New York: Pantheon, 1978.

Hewlett, Richard, and Francis Duncan. *Nuclear Navy, 1946–1962.* Chicago: University of Chicago Press, 1974.

Hoopes, Townsend, and Douglas Brinkley. *Driven Patriot: The Life and Times of James Forrestal.* New York: Knopf, 1992.

Kiepper, James. *Styles Bridges: Yankee Senator.* Sugar Hill, New Hampshire: Phoenix Publishing, 2001.

Levy, Herbert. *Henry Morgenthau, Jr.: The Remarkable Life of FDR's Secretary of the Treasury.* New York: Skyhorse, 2010.

Manchester, William. *American Caesar: Douglas MacArthur, 1880–1964.* Boston: Little, Brown, 1978.

McCullough, David. *Truman.* New York: Simon & Schuster, 1992.

McFarland, Keith, and David Roll. *Louis Johnson and the Arming of America: The Roosevelt and Truman Years.* Bloomington, Indiana: Indiana University Press, 2005.

Metcalf, Henry H., ed. *One Thousand New Hampshire Notables: Brief Biographical Sketches of New Hampshire Men and Women, Native or Resident, Prominent in Public, Professional, Business, Educational, Fraternal, or Benevolent Work.* Concord, New Hampshire: Rumford Printing Company, 1919.

Millis, Walter, ed. *The Forrestal Diaries.* New York: Viking, 1951.

Morgenthau, Henry III. *Mostly Morgenthaus: A Family History.* New York: Ticknor and Fields, 1991.

Morison, Elizabeth, and Elting Morison. *New Hampshire: A Bicentennial History.* New York: Norton, 1976.

Nizer, Louis. *My Life in Court.* Garden City, New York: Doubleday, 1961.

Pollack, Sheldon. *The Failure of U.S. Tax Policy: Revenue and Politics.* University Park, Pennsylvania: Pennsylvania State University Press, 1996.

Polmar, Norman, and Thomas Allen. *Rickover: Controversy and Genius.* New York: Simon and Schuster, 1982.

Schlesinger, Arthur M. Jr. *The Age of Roosevelt.* Vol. 2, *The Coming of the New Deal.* Boston: Houghton Mifflin, 1958.

Sheehan, Neil. *A Fiery Peace in a Cold War: Bernard Schriever and the Ultimate Weapon.* New York: Random House, 2009.

Smith, Jean Edward. *FDR*. New York: Random House, 2007.

Truman, Harry. *Memoirs of Harry S. Truman*. 2 vols. Garden City, New York: Doubleday, 1955–1956.

Walsh, David. *The Decline and Renaissance of the Navy, 1922–1944*. Committee on Naval Affairs, United States Senate. Washington, D.C.: Government Printing Office, 1944.

Weisband, Edward, and Thomas Franck. *Resignation in Protest: Political and Ethical Choices Between Loyalty to Team and Loyalty to Conscience in American Public Life*. New York: Grossman Publishers, 1975.

Westwood, Howard. *Burning Tree Club: A History: 1922–1962*. Bethesda, Maryland: Merkle Press, 1962.

Wright, James. *The Progressive Yankees: Republican Reformers in New Hampshire, 1906–1916*. Hanover, New Hampshire: University Press of New England, 1987.

ARTICLES AND PAPERS

Blakey, *The Revenue Act of 1941*, The American Economic Review, Vol. 31, No. 4 (Dec. 1941).

Blakey and Blakey, *The Two Federal Revenue Acts of 1940*, The American Economic Review, Vol. 30, No. 4 (Dec. 1940).

Dishman, *New Hampshire Limelight: The 1952 Kefauver-Truman Presidential Primary Campaign*, Historical New Hampshire, Vol. 42, no. 3, Fall 1987.

Kent, *The Revenue Act of 1940*, California Law Review, Vol. 29, pp. 160-184 (1941).

MAGAZINES, JOURNALS, AND NEWSPAPERS CONSULTED

*New York Times * Washington Post * The Washington Times * Manchester Union-Leader *Boston Globe * Boston Post * Baltimore Sun * Portsmouth Herald * Washington Times-Herald * Time * Newsweek * United States News * Army and Navy Journal*

U.S. GOVERNMENT AND CONGRESSIONAL PUBLICATIONS

The Historic Tables—Budget of the U.S. Government for 2012

Bickley, James. *War Bonds in the Second World War: A Model for a New Iraq/Afganistan War Bond?*, Congressional Research Service Report for Congress No. 7-5700, March 1, 2010.

Source Notes

Abbreviations Used

Acheson	Acheson, *Present at the Creation*
COASN	Coletta, *American Secretaries of the Navy*, vol. 2
COUSNDU	Coletta, *The United States Navy and Defense Unification, 1947–1953*
DJLS	John L. Sullivan diary/daily record
DP	Hoopes and Brinkley, *Driven Patriot*
FD	*The Forrestal Diaries*
FDRL	Franklin D. Roosevelt Presidential Library and Museum
Hess	Jerry Hess oral history interview with JLS, March 27, April 13, 1972
HSTL	Harry S. Truman Library and Museum
HSTMEM	*Memoirs of Harry S. Truman*
JLS	John L. Sullivan
LJAA	McFarland and Roll, *Louis Johnson and the Arming of America*
MUL	*Manchester Union-Leader*
Nizer	Nizer, *My Life in Court*
NYT	*New York Times*
PHM	Papers of Henry Morgenthau, Jr.
PJLS	Papers of John L. Sullivan
RICK	Polmar and Allen, *Rickover*
RIP	Weisband and Franck, *Resignation in Protest*
TRU	McCullough, *Truman*
WP	*Washington Post*

PART I: DEMOCRAT IN A REPUBLICAN STATE

Chapter One. Friendly Relationships on Both Sides of the Aisle

3–5 The men were in the living room: This scene is the actual portrayal from Connie Fields' detailed memory, author's interview.

Chapter Two. New Hampshire Nurturing

7–8 At the time Sullivan was born: HSTL, JLS Bio.; www. datesinhistory.com/; http://en.wikipedia.org/wiki/1899.

8–9 Manchester, New Hampshire, was itself: Blood, *Manchester on the Merrimack*, 13–291; Hareven and Langenbach, *Amoskeag*, 13–21.

9–10 John was very close: Patricia Meyers, author's interview.

10 Patrick Sullivan's parents: Marriage record, City of Cambridge, Massachusetts, October 30, 1865; *Cambridge Chronicle* obituary of Cornelius Sullivan (Julia's brother), October 2, 1907.

10 Entering the United States: Charles Sullivan, author's interview; Letter from Charles Sullivan to author dated November 10, 2009, with attachments including marriage record, City of Cambridge, Massachusetts.

10 Somewhere in the Sullivan DNA: See previous note; Metcalf, *One Thousand New Hampshire Notables*, 385.

11 Patrick married Ellen Harrington: Metcalf at 385.; marriage record, Nashua, New Hampshire.

11 He ran for the United States Congress: *Boston Daily Globe*, April 25, 1917, 6; May 25, 1917, 2; May 30, 1917, 1.

11 Both in his law: Patricia Meyers, author's interview.

11 Patrick and Nellie's first son: Patricia Meyers, author's interview; records of deaths, Manchester, New Hampshire.

11 At an early age: Patricia Meyers, James County, author's interviews.

12 In 1917 Sullivan entered Dartmouth College: Patricia Meyers, author's interview.

12 He left Dartmouth: Hess, 2; *Boston Sunday Post*, June 23, 1946, A-4.

12 "In World War I, I was anxious": Hess, 8; see previous note 23.

12 "We had eight members": see two previous notes and the subsequent story.

12–13 It is recorded that: Cincinnati *Times-Star*, December 24, 1945.

13 He graduated from Dartmouth in 1921: 1921 Dartmouth College Yearbook.

13–14   In the first two decades: Blood, *Manchester on the Merrimack*, 292–313; Hareven and Langenbach, *Amoskeag*, 21–25.

14   Patrick's early death: Patricia Meyers, author's interview.

14   John was determined: Ibid.

15   Captain Manning's son: Ibid.

15   Mary Carpenter Manning's maternal: Ibid.

15   Mary Carpenter Manning was widowed: Ibid.

15   Priscilla Manning: Ibid.

16   When Priscilla and John: Patricia Meyers, author's interview; Letter dated August 22, 1982, from Elizabeth Gilrain to Priscilla Sullivan.

16   Even though the Mannings: Patricia Meyers and Tedson Meyers, author's interviews.

16   When he finished law school: Patricia Meyers, author's interview.

16   During their courting: See previous note; WP June 14, 1945, p. 5C.

16   In his early years: See *Manchester Leader*, March 18, 1947, p. 1; American Legion entry at http://en.wikipedia.org/wiki/American_Legion.

17   Luckily for Sullivan: *Dartmouth Alumni Magazine*, March 1938.

17   Other than his two: Patricia Meyers, author's interview.

17   Bridges was born: Kiepper, *Styles Bridges*, 3–33.

18   Sullivan was a popular party leader: See previous note.

18   Both candidates directed: See two previous notes.; Patricia Meyers, author's interview.

19   Always one to find: *Boston Sunday Post*, June 23, 1946, p. A-4, cols. 4 and 5.

19   Two years later: Hess 2; Kiepper, *Styles Bridges*, 62-64.

19   When it was all over: See previous note.

19   Bridges would go on: Kiepper, *Styles Bridges*, 65–241.

20   John L. carefully edged: This scene is imagined, but both the author and Sullivan's daughter Patricia believe that it is an accurate representation of the development of Sullivan's thought processes and ambition in this period.

21   "What a young lawyer": John L. Sullivan, author's conversation.

PART II: WASHINGTON

Chapter Three. Connected: Assistant to the U.S. Commissioner of Internal Revenue

27   "The following week…": Hess, 2.

27 James A. Farley had the reputation: See http://en.wikipedia. org/wiki/James_Farley; Farley, *Jim Farley's Story*, pp 1-339.

28 "I told him…": Hess 2.

28 "right off the bat…": Hess 2.

Chapter Four. Assistant Secretary of the Treasury

29 On January 17, 1940, just over three months: Hess, 2–3.

29 Even before being sworn in: DJLS, January 2,4,5,8,9, 1940.

29–30 "Prisc[illa] at lunch at White House…": DJLS, February 6, 1940.

31 "When he [Sullivan]…": COASN, 748.

31 Sullivan's boss: Morgenthau, *Mostly Morgenthaus*, 213–439; Blum, *Years of War, 1938-1941*, 1-478; Levy, *Henry Morgenthau, Jr.*, 245-442.

32 In this respect: Lippmann, Today and Tomorrow, "Time for Some Resignations,"New York Herald Tribune, February 25, 1943.

32 John Sullivan helped filled these voids: Hess, 3, 13; COUSNDU, 26.

32 "[H]e went to Washington": COUSNDU, 26; See Norris, WP, June 16, 1946, B3.

33 "they were very, very close": Hess, 3.

33 "In the latter job": Norris, "New John L. Kayoes With Charm," WP, June 16, 1946, B3; DP, 356.

33 "John L. became very popular": See previous note.

33–34 Arthur Schlesinger, Jr.: Schlesinger, *The Coming of the New Deal*, 243.

34 An example of how: DJLS, January 24, 1940.

34 Almost immediately: DJLS, January–May 1940.

34 Sullivan was also: See previous note.

34 He began a long: See previous two notes.

35 Sullivan spent: See previous three notes.

35 As the likelihood: See previous four notes.

36 In the middle of May: DJLS, May 17, 1940.

36 Facing strong: Brands, *Traitor to His Class*, 512.

36 Then, on August 23: Brands, *Traitor to His Class*, 524-583; Smith, *FDR*, 434.

37 On April 9: Smith, *FDR*, 444.

37 On the same day: Id at 446.

37 The situation: Id at 447; Battle_of_Dunkirk, Wikipedia.org.

37 Roosevelt let it be known: Smith, *FDR* 446–47.

38 On June 10: Id at 448.

38 On June 19: Id at 449.

38-39   Frank Knox was one of Manchester, New Hampshire's: Beasley, *Frank Knox*, 1–184; COASN, 677–727.

40   Their options were limited: CRS Report to Congress, *Financing Issues and Economic Effects of American Wars, July 29, 1940.*

40   Treasury's preliminary calculations: Blakey and Blakey, *The Two Revenue Acts of 1940, pp. 724-726;* Pollack, *The Failure of U.S. Tax Policy,* pp 63-66;

41   By eight-thirty a.m.: DJLS, May 27, 1940.

41   Senator Harrison and Congressman Cooper: See previous note.

42   On Tuesday morning: DJLS, May 28, 1940.

42   At five-thirty p.m.: DJLS, May 28, 1940.

42   Sullivan headed: DJLS, May 29, 1940.

43   Within days after: DJLS, July 8, 1940.

44   The president gave: See previous note.

44   Later that evening: See two previous notes; DJLS, July 9–10, 1940.

44   Following drafting: See three previous notes.

45   A pertinent interlude... "Secretary Knox explained": DJLS, July 13, 1940.

45–46   In the following days: DJLS, July 15, 1940.

46   On July 23 Sullivan: DJLS, July 23, 1940.

46   The next week: DJLS, July 29, 1940.

46–47   The principal difference... "It penalizes defense...": See previous note.

47   On July 30: DJLS, July 30, 1940.

47   Sullivan and Morgenthau agreed... "the combining..." DJLS, August 2, 6, 1940.

47   Unexpectedly, it was: DJLS, August 10, 1940.

47   "Senator LaFollette seemed...": Ibid.

48   That same afternoon: See previous note.

48   On the following Monday: DJLS, August 12, 1940.

48   Sullivan then suggested... "I finally learned...": DJLS, August 23, 1940.

49   The next day, the president: DJLS, August 24, 1940.

49   The Democrats then proceeded: See previous note; DJLS, September 4, 1940.

49   Differences in the Senate: DJLS, September 4, 6, 9, 1940.

49   On September 11 both Sullivan: DJLS, September 11, 1940.

50   It was projected: Blakey and Blakey, *The Two Revenue Acts of 1940* 730.

50   When Jim Farley called: Farley, *Jim Farley's Story*, 192-298.

50   "Bill Bray called": DJLS, March 7, 1940.

51   At the Democratic convention: Smith, *FDR*, 456-480.

52   Both before and after: Id at 467–72.

52   After extensive political: This 1940 agreement should not be confused with the Lend-Lease Act of March 11, 1941, that authorized the president to "sell,, transfer title to, exchange, lease, lend, or otherwise dispose of, to any such [Allied] government any defense article." The act lasted throughout the war.

52   Over the protests: Smith, *FDR* 472–80.

52   Within days of: DJLS, November 20, 26, 1940.

53   At the White House dinner meeting: DJLS, November 28, 1940, and December 5, 1940.

53   Having received: DJLS, December 5, 1940.

54   During the following week: DJLS, December 6, 1940.

54   On January 23: DJLS, January 22, 23, 1941.

54   Sullivan was inundated: DJLS, February and March 1941; Treasury press release, February 10, 1941.

54   On March 4: DJLS, March 4, 5, 1941; Draft Morgenthau letter to FDR, March 17, 1941.

54–55 During this same period: DJLS, April 8, 16, 1941.

55   Sullivan and Morgenthau met alone: DJLS, April 11, 1941.

55   "After we arose...": See previous note.

55   During the months: DJLS, April, May, and June 1941.

56   On April 24... "[F]irst, that the...": JLS statement to House Ways and Means Committee, April 24, 1941.

56   On May 19: JLS statement to House Ways and Means Committee, May 19,1941 (see Appendix A).

56   By the beginning: DJLS, June 2, 3, 4, 1941; WP, "Treasury Gets 2-3d Revenue Payment Plan," June 3, 1941.

57   On June 9: DJLS, June 9, 10, 11, 12, 13, 1941.

57   A week later President Roosevelt: DJLS, July 15, 1941.

57–58 Later on the same day... "Complete secrecy...": WP, "Heavier Taxes Due Next Year, Roosevelt Says," July 16, 1941.

58   Discussion apparently languished: DJLS, July 30, 1941.

58–59 The president began... "He would like...": See previous note

60   Following the White House: See two previous notes.

61   During the first week: JLS statement to Senate Finance Committee, August 8, 1941 (see Appendix B).

61   The Senate worked: DJLS, September 5, 16, 17, 20, 1941.

62   But the Treasury team: WP, November 6, 1941, 1.

62–63 Following church on Sunday... "With a few appropriate remarks...": Westwood, *Burning Tree Club*, 78–79.

63   Sullivan's job had just intensified: Jerry Kluttz, Federal Diary, WP, December 16, 1941; August 4, 1942, 5; and March 23, 1944, 9.

63   ...an eminent New York lawyer, Randolph: See Blum, *Years of Urgency, 1938-1941*, 290, 293,315-318. Paul's own contribution in revising the tax code and raising revenues was substantial and has been widely recognized.

63   At this point the Roosevelt Administration: Gabler, *Walt Disney*, 384–86.

64   "I find it difficult": JLS letter to Walt Disney, January 26, 1942.

65   The first of these: WP, May 1, 1941, 1; DJLS memo of December 12, 1941.

65   On December 22: DJLS, December 22, 1941.

66   On Saturday, January 3: DJLS, January 3, 9, 11, 1942.

66   In a speech: WP, January 20, 1942, 2.

66   On January 24: DJLS, January 24, 31, 1942.

67   On several occasions: DJLS, December 10, 1941, and February 9, 12, 1942.

67   On February 20: DJLS, February 20, 1942.

67   In April: DJLS, April 27, 28, 1942, and May 6, 20, 1942. See also "Working Arrangement on War Contract Cases" included in Truman Library file of diary entries.

67   On May 28: See May 28 statement attached to diary entry of same date.

67   On June 14: JLS speech to UN Flag Day Rally in Chicago, Illinois, June 14, 1942 (see Appendix D).

67   Sullivan frequently: See, for example, DJLS, July 3, 1942.

67–68   Developing a plan: JLS memo to Morgenthau, August 28, 1942.

68   Sullivan spoke about: DJLS, August 26, 1942, and September 28, 1942.

68   During October: See, for example, DJLS, October 7, 1942; NYT, October 30, 1942, 1; WP, October 30, 1942, 1; November 10, 1942, 17; and January 26, 1942; Memo—"Regulation of War Contracts" 1944 included in Truman Library file of diary entries.

68   In December he was consumed: DJLS, December 7, 1942; January 12, 15, 26, 1943; February 10, 1943; March 9, 1943; and June 19, 1943.

68   On December 9, 1943: See Dow Jones release, December 10, 1942, 1:12 p.m. included in Truman Library file with December 9 diary entries.

68   On December 14: DJLS, December 14, 1942.

68–69   In February 1943: DJLS, February 15, 1943.

69   In 1943 Sullivan: DJLS, January 26, 29, 1943, see, for example, telephone conference with Dr. Gallup, March 9, 1943; WSJ, March 6, 1943, 1.

69   Regarding tax collecting: *United States News*, March 12, 1943.

69   "You'd be surprised at how": *Washington Times-Herald*, October 20, 1943.

69–70   He was also: DJLS, March 5, 11, 12, 17, 23, 1943; Memorandum— "Reasons Why," in same Truman Library file of diary entries.

70   At the end of May: DJLS, May 27, 1943, and June 2, 16, 1943.

70   On June 11: JLS memo to the secretary, June 11, 1943.

70   In mid-August: DJLS, August 11, 12, 1943.

70   On September 8: WP, September 8, 1943, 1.

71   "Ten years ago": *Collier's* magazine, November 6, 1943.

71   In late 1943: Draft of Minutes of Joint Contract Termination Board, November 24, 1943, and memo from JLS to Secretary Morgenthau, December 31, 1943.

71   On December 29: DJLS, December 29, 1943.

71   In January, 1944: See, for example, Minutes of Second Meeting of the SWPPB, March 9, 1944; WP, February 24, 1944, 7.

71   In the summer of 1944: *Manchester Leader*, June 12, 1944.

72   By Labor Day: JLS memoranda to Secretary Morgenthau, September 25, 1944, and October 3, 1944.

72   One day in 1943 he had occasion: Laurence Connell, author's interview.

72   The second story: Deborah DuSault, author's interview.

72   A third tale: James County, author's interview.

73   While he was serving: Patricia Meyers, author's interview.

73   Six weeks after: Westwood, *Burning Tree Club*, 78–79.

73   Harry Truman had become: TRU, 253–91.

73   Sullivan concurred: Hess, 4.

73   As the Democratic convention: TRU, 292–324.

73   "I think it was a case of God": Hess, 4.

73   "I wasn't sorry": Ibid.

73   "I got the word": Ibid.

74   "I hadn't seen him since": Hess, 5.

74   "I discovered early on": JLS to author.

74   When his daughter: Author's interview with Deborah DuSault.

74   Priscilla Sullivan, by nature: Patricia Meyers and Deborah DuSault, author's interviews.

75   Three years after he left: Photograph in HSTL; Navy Department release, February 6, 1947.

75   World War II had cost: The Historic Tables—Budget of the U.S. Government for 2012, p. 139.

75   . . . seven war bond campaigns . . . $186 billion: See http:/www. economy-world-war-ii-aaw-03/ and Bickley, *War Bonds in the Second World War: A Model for a New Iraq/Afganistan War Bond?*, Congressional Research Report for Congress, March 1, 2010.

Chapter Five. Assistant Secretary of the Navy for Air

77   During the 1944: Smith, *FDR*, 625–26.

77   Sullivan resigned as . . . 'because' ": Hess, 5; DJLS, November 15, 1944; Letter from JLS to Morgenthau, November 15, 1944; Letter from Morgenthau to JLS, November 15, 1944; Letter from JLS to President Roosevelt dated December 1, 1944, but delivered November 15, 1944; Letter from Roosevelt to JLS, November 27, 1944.

77   He did not mention: See Drew Pearson column, *New York Herald-Tribune*, November 15, 1944, and Jerry Kluttz, Federal Diary, WP, November 28, 1944.

77   Earlier in the year: See Jerry Kluttz, Federal Diary, WP, June 14, 1944; DJLS, November 15, 1944.

78   "The Senatorial thing": JLS letter to William D. Horne, dated June 13. 1944.

78   He then also declined: DJLS, November 15, 1944.

78   "On the day of the…": Hess, 5–6.

79   He said, "Assistant Secretary…": DP 188.

80   "I immediately went over to the Navy": Hess, 7.

80   He made immediate arrangements: *Boston Sunday Post*, June 23, 1946, p. A-4.

80   "Hi, John L.! How's the hook?": Id at col. 1.

81   "They [the people on the Hill] all knew": Hess, 13.

81   "Well, you see, President Roosevelt": Ibid.

82   As assistant secretary for air: NYT, September 23, 1945, 6.

Chapter Six. Undersecretary of the Navy

83   "In the same Navy Department": David Lawrence, "Public Office is a Public Trust," *United States News*, February 15, 1946, 29.

84   In attendance at Sullivan's: *Boston Sunday Post*, June 23, 1946, p. A-4.

84   Robert Patterson, secretary of war… "severely against…": Hess, 11–12.

85   Sullivan immediately took charge: Ibid.

85 By the end of 1946, fueled by warnings from the likes: Acheson, *Present at The Creation* 217-235.

86 "If we throw away": COUSNDU, 45.

86 It was no secret: Acheson, *Present at the Creation* 220-235.

86 In early February, President Truman: Hess, 14.

86 "[E]verybody on the Hill": Ibid.

87 "When the President learned": Ibid.

87 On March 7 the president called: Acheson, *Present at the Creation* 221.

87 On March 12 the president: Id at 221-222.

87 "I believe that it must be the policy": Id at 222.

88 During the next three months: Id at 221-223.

88 Finally, in May the Congress: Id at 223; Public Law 75, 80th Congress, Chapter 81, 1st Session, S. 938, May 22, 1947.

88 Truman was later quoted . . . "the greatest selling job": See http://www.answers.com/topic/truman-doctrine-2.

88 That same month: TRU, 561–563.

88 "I think the Marshall Plan received": Hess, 15.

89 In November 1943: Caraley, *The Politics of Military Unification*, 23.

89 ". . . unthinkable [that all the military forces]": *Baltimore Sun*, June 7, 1946.

90 He repeated: Ibid.

90 Even before passage: COUSNDU, 57.

90 The Navy leadership immediately: Id at 54–57.

90 Independent analyses... "At a time when...": COUSNDU, 39.

91 Sullivan insisted: COUSNDU, 31.

91 The Secretary of the Navy: Ibid.

Chapter Seven. Secretary of the Navy

93–94 "John L. Sullivan gave me...": *Washington Times-Herald*, September 28, 1947; *Chicago Herald-American*, September 29, 1947.

95–96 James V. Forrestal was an extraordinary: DP, 115-364.

96 John Sullivan served: COUSNDU, 17, 28; COASN, 747–52; DP, 358–59.

96 "My father and I had been": Hess, 8.

97 "He was a first-class fellow": Hess, 22.

98 "This thing [unification] is going to work.": COUSNDU, 29.

98 A Navy historian concluded: Id at 27.

98 At the time Sullivan took over: Id at 29.

98–99 "Thereafter he delegated...": Ibid.

99 Even at the start of his tenure: Id at 45.

99	Senator Harry Truman: Id at 17.
99	He concluded that the military: Ibid.
99	Later, in his *Memoirs*… "It was inevitable…": HSTMEM, vol. 2, 34.
100	When he did become president: COUSNDU, 20.
100	"In the fall of 1947…": Hess, 29–30.
102	Also to save money: COUSNDU, 46.
102	"I concur": Id at 32.
102	On November 13: Henry Beauregard memo to the secretary of the Navy dated November 11, 1947.
102	The battle among: DP, 365–68.
102	"It has been made clear…": Chief of Naval Operations Nimitz memo to Secretary of the Navy Sullivan dated October 13, 1947.
104	A major aspect: DP, 365–68.
104	Sullivan was taken aback: COUSNDU, 46–47, 54–56.
104	"On May 5, 1948…": Id at 47.
104	Sullivan lost a strong aide: Id at 41, 54; COASN, 754.
104	Symington replied: COUSNDU, 57.
105	"It is time right now…": Ibid.
105	Privately he may well have: DP, 370.
105	Sullivan was provoked sufficiently: COUSNDU, 93.
105	As a successor to Nimitz: COASN, 752.
105	Forrestal, after obtaining: COUSNDU, 65–66; COASN, 758–60.
106	Suffice it to say: COUSNDU, 68.
106	In the interim, on March 25: WP, March 26, 1948.
106	On June 24, 1948: DP, 365–68.
107	On August 20 to 22, 1948: COUSNDU, 80–83; COASN, 764–65; DP, 410–12.
107	"the Navy should be equipped…": DP, 411.
107	In May 1948 a long-time: COASN, 766–71; DP, 321–22.
107	"air should be an integral part": COUSNDU, 105.
107–08	The committee report: COUSNDU, 107–10.
108	"How could one discuss": Id at 110.
108	The National Security Council created: Id at 20–21.
108	Sullivan's view was: Hess, 20–21.
109	(Undoubtedly he felt that way…): Hess 20.
109	In 1947 and the early part: DP, 387–404.
109	To add to the pressure: DP, 415–21; COUSNDU, 58–59; JLS letter to Johnson, April 23, 1949.
110	Truman went along: COUSNDU, 59–60.
110	Symington, however: Ibid.

110–12 His testimony was summarized... "[Sullivan] noted...": COUSNDU, 116–17.

112 On March 10, Drew Pearson: WP, March 10, 1949.

112 "Forrestal now believed...": DP, 424.

113 ...on January 11, 1949, Truman: DP, 438.

113 On March 28 he was: DP, 446.

113 His emotional tailspin: DP, 447–63.

113 On May 22, at age fifty-seven: DP, 464–65.

113 "the passing of this distinguished...": DP, 466.

Chapter Eight. Nuclear Navy: The Decision to Build the USS Nautilus

115 At one fifty-five in the afternoon: Author's discussions with JLS and Admiral Robert Carney.

115 Even before the end: RICK, 115–34; COUSNDU, 38; Hewlett and Duncan, *Nuclear Navy*, 10–12.

115 While Fleet Admiral Ernest King: RICK, 127; Hewlett and Duncan, *Nuclear Navy*, 1–28.

116 From 1946 to 1947: Hewlett and Duncan, *Nuclear Navy*, 28–51.

116 The difficulties facing: Ibid., 44–56.

116 Notwithstanding his own prickly personality: Ibid., 57, 77; RICK, 138.

117 Sullivan waved the admirals... "Gentlemen, for some weeks...": Author's discussions with JLS and Admiral Robert Carney. As to the relevant follow-on documentation, see three memoranda: Nimitz to Sullivan, Dec. 5, 1947; Sullivan to Forrestal, Dec. 8, 1947; Sullivan to Bush, Dec. 8, 1947; and Sulllivan to Mills and P.F. Lee, Dec. 8, 1947 (all in Naval Reactors Division). See also Mills to Lilienthal, Aug. 2, 1948 (AEC records); Mills to Sullivan, Aug. 3, 1948; first endorsement, Denfield to Sullivan, Aug. 3, 1948; and Sullivan to Forrestal, Aug. 4, 1948 (last three all in Naval Reactors Division). The precise date of Sullivan's meeting with the admirals is a best estimate based on diary entries.

117 Secretary Forrestal agreed: Hewlett and Duncan, *Nuclear Navy*, 57, 77.

118 "The potentialities of atomic energy": Hess, 19.

118 The project resulted in: RICK, 164.

118 Immediately the *Nautilus*: RICK, 165–79.

118 A total of 198: United States Navy information office.

119 Years later, in the mid-1960s: Author's discussions with JLS and Admiral Robert Carney.

129 On April 4, 1949: Id at 131.

129 "We had laid the keel…": Hess, 25.

130 The contract for the construction: MUL, April 27, 1949.

130 On April 21 Secretary of the Army: COUSNDU, 134.

130 On April 22 Sullivan testified: Ibid.

130 Immediately after his testimony: Id at 134–35.

130 While he was there: Id at 135.

130 When advised: Ibid.

130 Rushing to the Pentagon: Hess 42.

131 "Are you determined to resign?": RIP 45; Hess 26–27.

135 "Sullivan has joined..": COUSNDU 136.

135 Johnson made public: Barlow 211-213 and supporting footnotes at 525-26.

135 Johnson did not even receive: Ibid.

135 On December 28 "…Personally, I believe…": Ibid.

136 He confirmed "Van[denberg] will not agree…": Ibid.

136 "Whether the Joint Chiefs…" COUSNDU 141.

136 In fact Johnson had made up his mind: Barlow 212, 526, fn. 96.

136 When questioned by a historian: Hess, 30.

136 Later in the evening: RIP 63, 91.

136–37 It was documented.: Ibid. The original ten cited by Weisband and Franck, authors of *Resignation in Protest*, were Harold Ickes, Webster Davis, William Jennings Bryan, Lewis Douglas, Henry Wallace, Lindley Garrison, Henry Breckenridge, Walter Hickel, Kenneth Davis, and John Sullivan. Later Elliot Richardson and William Ruckleshaus added themselves to the group by reason of their conduct after the Nixon "Saturday Night Massacre" in October 1973.

137 "There are dramatic…" RIP 91.

137 On May 3 Sullivan: COUSNDU 142.

137–38 "A boatsman's mate piped…": NYT, May 24 1949.

138–39 "Sullivan's resignation immediately became…": LJAA 175.

139 The media and public reaction: COUSNDU 138–43.

139 President Truman later told: LJAA 187; TRU 741.

139 Sullivan's resignation, in protest: COUSNDU 169–227; LJAA 168–87.

139 In congressional hearings: Ibid.

140 "The creation of three departments…": Id at 176–77.

140 John Sullivan's successor: COUSNDU 149–68.

141 At six o'clock in the morning: Sheehan, *A Fiery Peace in a Cold War* 99.

141   The Navy never abandoned: COUSNDU, 297–317; United States Navy Information Office.

141   These vessels are now dubbed: Ibid.

143   "After [his] mercurial blast…": RIP 45–46.

143   It was Louis Johnson's own: COUSNDU 229–328.

143–44 "[Johnson's political ambition] was evident…": Id at 137.

144   Riley's judgment was confirmed: Manchester, *American Caesar* 532.

144   (During his time…): Hess 36.

PART III: LIFE ON THE OUTSIDE AGAIN

Chapter Eleven. Respected, Behind the Scenes

147   After his resignation: Author's own direct knowledge; author's discussions with JLS.

147–48 The firm was a most: Author's own remembrances.

148   Notwithstanding the firm's small size: Ibid.

149   The story of how: Author's discussions with JLS.

150–51 "When I left the Navy": Hess 32–33.

151   Sullivan was also sought: NYT, August 11, 1982.

151   One story: Bert Whittemore, author's interview.

152   In 1951 Sullivan: Author's discussion with JLS.

152   As the year 1952: TRU, 887–90.

152   "I thought that it was very important": Hess, 33.

152   Sullivan proceeded with: Ibid.

152   During the primary period: Hess, 34; TRU, 891–92.

152   Sullivan raised: *Historical New Hampshire.* Fall 1987, 233, 235.

152   Consequently, on March 11 Kefauver: Ibid.; Hess, 33.

152   Truman's aides: NYT, March 14, 1952.

152   The president's other advisers: TRU, 892.

153–54 "My decision not to be a candidate…": HSTMEM, Vol. Two 488-89.

154   After the 1946 midterm elections: The Twenty-second Amendment to the Constitution states: "Section 1. No person shall be elected to the office of the President more than twice, and no person who has held the office of President, or acted as President, for more than two years of a term to which some other person was elected President shall be elected to the office of the President more than once. But this article shall not apply to any person holding the office of President when this article was proposed by the Congress, and shall not prevent any person who may be holding

the office of President, or acting as President, during the term within which this article becomes operative from holding the office of President or acting as President during the remainder of such term.

"Section 2. This article shall be inoperative unless it shall have been ratified as an amendment to the Constitution by the legislatures of three-fourths of the several States within seven years from the date of its submission to the States by the Congress."

154   While the campaign slogged on: TRU, 893–903.

154   There Kefauver led in delegates: TRU, 903–6.

154   Sullivan attended the convention: Hess, 33, 34.

155   "I worked very hard": Hess, 34.

155   The 1952 race was the last: NYT, August 11, 1982.

155   He remained an active sportsman: Patricia Meyers, author's interview; author's own direct knowledge.

155   On one occasion: Author's discussion with JLS.

156   Another Burning Tree story: Ibid.

156   Sullivan was the quintessential: Ibid.; author's own direct knowledge; author's discussions with JLS.

156   In the 1940s Loews: Nizer, 427–523.

157   Sullivan continued to maintain: Author's discussions with JLS; Patricia Meyers, author's interview.

157   In the late 1950s and early 1960s: Peter Fuller, author's interview.

157   He and Priscilla spent: Patricia Meyers and Deborah DuSault, author's interviews.

158   Sullivan was a member: JLS papers at Dartmouth's Rauner Special Collections Library.

158   Dartmouth, the University of New Hampshire…: Ibid.

158   He continued to be held: Author's discussion with JLS.

158   After awhile the bulk: Patricia Meyers, author's interview; author's own direct knowledge.

158   He died of a heart attack: Obituaries in the WP, NYT, and MUL, August 11, 1982.

158   Soon after John's death: Patricia Meyers and Deborah DuSault, author's interviews.

158–59 "Contrary to widespread belief…": George Dixon, *Washington Times-Herald*, September 28, 1947.

APPENDICES

A. Statement of JLS before House Ways and Means Committee, May 19, 1941.
B. Statement of JLS before the Senate Finance Committee, August 8, 1941.
C. JLS speech to General Assembly of Virginia, January 19, 1942, Richmond, Virginia.
D. JLS speech to United Nations Flag Day Rally in Chicago, Illinois, on June 14, 1942 (War Bonds).
E. JLS testimony to House Committee on Appropriations Subcommittee, February 16, 1949.

APPENDIX A

STATEMENT OF JOHN L. SULLIVAN, ASSISTANT SECRETARY
OF THE TREASURY, BEFORE THE COMMTTEE ON WAYS
AND MEANS OF THE HOUSE OF REPRESENTATIVES,
MONDAY, MAY 19, 1941

* * *

My purpose today is to discuss with you the problem of corporate taxation in the present emergency. What I shall have to say is supplementary to the statement made by Secretary Morgenthau when the current hearings were opened and to the suggestions laid before you subsequently on behalf of the Treasury Department.

The Treasury is called upon to meet expenditures greater than have ever been made in the nation's peacetime history, and probably greater than at any period in our history, in peace or war. At such a time we cannot expect to rely on normal sources of revenue or be content with revenue in normal amounts. We must adopt extraordinary measures to deal with our extraordinary situation.

Your committee is now formulating changes in our tax system, both to provide the revenues needed to finance the defense expenditures that we are committed to make, and also to assist in maintaining the economic health of the nation. Our people knew that great sacrifices must be made and they are prepared to make them. They rely upon you so to plan our financial program that, however severe its burdens may have to be, they will rest fairly and justly upon all individuals and all businesses.

The tax program which you will propose will necessarily consist of many elements. Any one tax, viewed by itself, may appear to be stringent. All must be viewed, however, as parts of a whole. This is an emergency. Taxes that would not be proposed in normal times are a necessity now.

I have been asked particularly to discuss the excess profits tax, first enacted in the fall of 1940. Our experience with it is still limited, for many of the returns of the largest corporations have not yet been filed. Enough have been filed, however, to convince

185

Treasury officials in charge of tax administration that important changes in the law must be made in the interests of fairness. We are collecting large sums by means of this tax, but the profits of a good many firms are not being touched by the tax, although some of those profits are excess profits by any reasonable standard. Here is certainly a place to broaden the base. Surely the skill of this Committee and its experts is adequate to the task of bringing within the tax the known cases of corporate excess profits.

I want first to outline the principles which I believe should govern the taxation of excess profits; second, to indicate respects in which the present law fails to accord with those principles; and third, to suggest possible remedies which the Congress may wish to consider.

I- Principles

Under present conditions some kinds of profits may be appropriately subjected to heavier taxation than other kinds. This may be necessary in order to distribute the burden fairly and to avoid unfavorable economic effects that might result if the revenue were raised in other ways.

1. Defense profits

The first type of profits which, in a period of this kind, should be subjected to special taxation comprises the profits which may be reasonably attributed to the defense program. Such profits are being made out of the sacrifices of the people as a whole and should be returned to the people in taxes, insofar as may be possible without destroying necessary incentives to produce defense goods.

In many cases it is not possible to identify with precision the additional profits due to the defense program. The effects of defense spending are diffused throughout the whole economic system. It is necessary, accordingly, to assume that in general, increases in profits during this period are due to defense. Inability to measure defense profits precisely should not discourage us from subjecting them to special taxation even at the risk of hitting some income not derived from the defense program.

2. Profits in excess of a necessary normal return on invested capital

The other kind of profit that can properly be subjected to special taxation comprises profits in excess of a necessary normal return on invested capital, even if this return was being earned in the years prior to the defense program. The existence of such profits, while often due primarily to good management, is in numerous cases due to monopoly, imperfect competition, or service to the public. When as a result of the imperfections of our economic machinery such excess profits have been made, it is equitable and desirable that they be subjected to special taxation. Furthermore, at a time when heavy taxes must be imposed they should be levied where they will assist best in maintaining a well-functioning economy. To take an additional share of the profits in excess of a normal return on invested capital will not cause any companies to go into bankruptcy or withdraw from business.

I am aware that the anticipation of extraordinarily large profits may in many cases have put security prices well above a figure that would represent invested capital. The imposition of these special taxes may seem harsh to individuals who have purchased those securities at such levels. We must remember that no legislation is ever passed and no progressive step is ever taken which does not disturb expectations of some people. We submit that established expectations of high profits are entitled to no more protection than an individual's expectation of a continued large salary which is now to be subjected to a much heavier tax. This is an emergency, and changes must be expected.

I am also aware that the application of the principle of taxing profits in excess of a necessary normal return on capital involves difficulties of both principle and technique. These difficulties should not be underestimated, but I feel sure that we should not allow them to stand in the way of our seeking to attain the main objective.

II – Defects of the present law

In the light of the principles just stated, let us now examine the excess profits tax law passed last year, to see in what respects, if any, it fails to correspond to them.

1. Failure to reach large parts of defense profits

The Excess Profits Tax Act of 1940 was a clear expression of Congressional intent that profits growing out of the defense effort should be subject to excess profits tax.

The law, however, has not achieved that objective.

Many corporations that are the principal beneficiaries of the defense effort and that hold large government contracts are paying little or no profits tax.

In the absence of complete excess profits tax returns an examination has been made of published financial data for certain corporations. One company whose profits in 1940 were more than 3,000 percent larger than in 1939 is subject to no excess profits tax whatever on 1940 earnings and this is a company which has thus far received over $70 million of defense contracts. A large industrial company which has received over $250 million of defense contracts and had earnings in 1940 of nearly 200 percent larger than in 1939 will pay no excess profits tax. It appears that only 5 out of 12 large integrated steel companies will be subject to excess profits tax on the income of 1940, although steel companies have in general received huge amounts of defense orders.

These companies pay little or no excess profits tax because they are allowed a minimum credit of 8 percent of invested capital.

2. Failure to tax profits in excess of a necessary normal return

Another serious shortcoming of the 1940 excess profits tax law is that profits in excess of a necessary normal return on invested capital are not subject to the tax unless such profits also represent an increase over the profits of the base period. Companies which earned during the base period an average of 30 percent, 50 percent or even more on their present invested capital will be free from the excess profits tax on income in any year equal to approximately these percents and will be taxable only on increases in their incomes.

This failure of the law to reach a large portion of excess profits is due to the provision of a credit for every corporation equal to 95 percent of its base period earnings, regardless of the size of those earnings in relation to its invested capital.

III – Remedies

Revisions of the excess profits tax to be considered adequate, must reach the two kinds of profits which I have been discussing. The tax can reach a much larger proportion of defense profits if there is a reduction in the 8 percent credit on invested capital. Profits in excess of a necessary normal return can be reached by taxing all profits above a stated percentage of invested capital, regardless of average base period earnings.

These were the basic elements of the Treasury excess profits tax proposal of 1940, and it is this plan, with modifications dictated by experience, that we suggest. In that proposal corporations were to be allowed free of the excess profits tax an amount of earnings equal to their earnings during the base period, but not more than 10 percent of invested capital. However, they were granted a minimum credit of 4 percent of invested capital with 6 percent allowed on the first $500,000. Thus, under that plan a concern which earned 7 percent during the base period would be allowed to continue to earn 7 percent free of tax. A concern which earned only 2 percent during the base period would be permitted to earn 4 percent free of tax. A concern which earned 15 percent during the base period would be allowed to earn 10 percent free of tax.

Under the 1940 Treasury proposal it was recognized that if business is to expand and investors are to put money into new corporations, an opportunity must be allowed to earn an adequate rate of return on new capital. The plan allowed an 8 percent return on new capital, with a 10 percent return up to $500,000, regardless of the earnings experience during the base period on old capital.

If the plan submitted by the Treasury last year had been applied to the examples previously presented, the tax results would have been quite different. For example, one corporation which had a 30 percent return on its invested capital in the base period would have paid excess profits tax on over half of its 1940 income instead of on one-twelfth as under the present law. Another with a slightly lower rate of return would also have paid on over half instead of on one-fifth of its income. The large industrial company which received over $250 million of defense contracts would have paid excess profits tax on over one-third of its income and the other company with poor earnings in the base period would have paid on about one-fifth of its income instead of both companies being entirely exempt.

Even this plan, however, would have failed to reach substantial amounts of defense profits received by corporations which had especially poor earnings during the base period. To meet this defect we would suggest revising the 1940 proposal to provide that where the average earnings of the base period were less than the minimum of 4 percent, the excess profits tax should be applied at a low flat rate, possibly 10 percent, to that part of the current profits that is in excess of the base period earnings but not in excess of 4 percent of invested capital. For example, if a corporation earned during the base period an average of $100,000 a year, while 4 percent of its invested capital amounts to $300,000, the first $100,000 of profits in the current taxable year would be entirely exempt from excess profits tax, the next $200,000, representing the difference between the $100,000 average earnings and the $300,000 credit on invested capital, would be taxed at 10 percent and any earnings over $300,000 would be subject to the regular excess profits tax rates. This minimum rate of tax would subject all increases in profits during the defense period at least to some excess profits taxation without unduly burdening concerns whose increased earnings are not truly defense profits.

We would suggest also that the rate allowed on new capital be the same as that originally suggested, namely, 8 percent, with 10 percent for additions to capital that do not bring the total invested capital above $500,000. Any maximum return on capital must be a somewhat arbitrary figure because businesses differ widely in the degree of risk they face. Accordingly, it is desirable not to set too low a maximum rate of return.

Similarly, it would be desirable to keep the tax rate low on that part of profits which is immediately above the credit. To this end we suggest that tax rates be graduated in accordance with the rate of return on invested capital starting with a moderate initial rate.

Moreover, with this new broad excess profits base, it would be possible to adapt ourselves quickly and much more easily to a need for still larger revenues if the emergency should so require. The future is especially uncertain during an emergency period, and we might have to act quickly. It is better to have a broad excess profits tax base carefully worked out while we still have the time than to patch up the present law and take the risk of finding ourselves confronted with the necessity of improvising such a base on short notice at a later date.

Thus far I have outlined the principles of excess profits taxation which in our opinion should be followed in this emergency period and have indicated ways in which the existing law fails to carry them out. If you share our belief in these principles, I believe you will agree that a plan like the one I have outlined is the logical method of putting the principles into practical operation. Variation in details is not a matter of concern, so long as the plan adopted taxes both defense profits and excess profits, which the present law does not.

IV. Possible alternative

If these principles are not to be the guide for taxing corporations during the emergency period, it would be well to bear in mind the disadvantages of the tax in its present form, which involves the administrative difficulties inevitably accompanying excess profits taxation but fails to tax larger amounts of profits that it properly should reach. A simpler, more easily administered plan would, of course, be to abandon the excess profits tax and to increase the corporation income tax by enough to produce the desired revenue. With such an increase in the corporation income tax there should, in my judgment, be coupled a provision for reducing the tax when the earnings of the corporation are immediately made subject to the individual income tax.

This kind of a plan would be in harmony with the idea of integrating the corporation and the individual taxes, placing chief reliance on the taxation of income of individuals. Profiting from our experience with previous plans of this general character, many difficulties met can very likely be avoided and equitable taxation of profits to the individual stockholder provided.

I do not set forth this plan as one that carries into effect the principles which I previously discussed. It is based on principles of its own and is suggested as an alternative, not a substitute.

When I first appeared before the Committee in executive session and discussed this tax program with you generally, I told you that I thought there were certain types of durable commodities, such as electric refrigerators, automobiles, watches, clocks, and cameras, the reduced consumption of which would be helpful to national defense, not only because the plants are adaptable to defense work, but also because the materials used in these commodities are used in defense articles and the workmen who manufacture these things are possessed of the very skills that are needed in many of our defense plants. During that first discussion different members of the Committee expressed the view that taxes on some of these articles should be higher than were recommended and I assured them that we would not object to some increases on these particular articles. Since that time there has been so much discussion about various excess taxes that I think I should repeat to you what I said before—that I do believe these articles are the type that it is highly desirable to tax not only for revenue but also to reduce demands for goods which compete with the defense program.

We cannot expect to devise a painless tax bill. The situation calls for sacrifices.

As Secretary Morgenthau has already told you, we have had unmistakable evidence that the people are willing to make sacrifices according to their ability. Outside the tax field greater sacrifices are being asked and cheerfully made. There is no basis for comparing the sacrifices of those who are asked to exchange the security of a job and a home for a soldier's pay and a soldier's hardships with the sacrifices of those who are asked to pay drastically higher rates of tax.

APPENDIX B

Statement of John L. Sullivan,
Assistant Secretary of the Treasury,
before the Senate Finance Committee,
August 8, 1941.

In his discussion of taxation as an essential part of national defense, Secretary Morgenthau emphasized the need for paying a large proportion of the defense costs from present taxes and the need for making full use of the potentialities of the tax system in resisting price inflation. In the final analysis, the job of defense is largely a production job. The tax system, therefore, must be designed to enhance and not burden defense output. The job of defense is also one of national unity. This makes it imperative that as far as possible the huge tax burden necessitated by the emergency be apportioned among the various groups of our population equitably and without discrimination.

The Secretary has laid before you the broad outlines of our tax problem. My statement will deal more directly with the provisions of the pending bill.

In the Secretary's statement before the Ways and Means Committee he indicated a need for legislation to produce annually $3,500,000,000 additional revenue. This recommendation was based on the conclusion that current taxes should provide approximately two-thirds of the Federal expenditures during the emergency period. In terms of the fiscal year 1942 revenue and expenditures indicated last April, $3,500,000,000 additional revenue would have met the 2/3-1/3 ratio of taxes to borrowing.

In the past three months, the fiscal situation has undergone further change. Expenditures for the fiscal year 1942 are now estimated at $22,169,000,000 rather than the $19,000,000,000 as of April 24. Receipts from the existing revenue system would still be $1.9 billion short of the 2/3-1/3 goal.

This Bill, H.R. 5417, is estimated to produce in a year of full operation $3,236.7 million, or $263.3 million less than the amount recommended by the Secretary. Of this total, $864.8 million or 26.7 percent of the additional revenues will be derived from increases in individual income taxes, $1,345.2 million or 41.6 percent from increases in corporation taxes, $151.9 million or 4.7 percent from increases in estate and gift taxes and $874.8 million or 27.0 percent from new excises and increases in existing excises.

With respect to individual income tax, the provisions of the bill are confined principally to increases in the tax rates. The present rate of the normal income tax is unchanged, but the surtax rates are increased substantially. Moreover, the surtax under the revised schedule applies to the first dollar of surtax net income, whereas under existing law the first $4,000 of surtax income is free from surtax. The bill provides for increases in the surtax rather than in the normal tax, in order to place some of the additional tax burden on the recipients of interest from partially tax-exempt securities.

The rate schedule under the bill differs in certain respects from that proposed to the Ways and Means Committee by the Treasury. The bill imposes a tax of 5 percent upon the first $2,000 of surtax income and increases existing rates up to those applicable to $750,000. The Treasury recommended that the surtax start at 11 percent on the first $2,000 of surtax net income. Because of the importance of curbing the present inflationary tendency and because of the revenue it would produce, the Treasury repeats its recommendation.

The pending bill leaves the amount of the personal exemptions and the credit for dependents unchanged. The Revenue Act of 1940 decreased the exemptions from $1,000 to $800 for a single person and from $2,500 to $2,000 for a married couple. Approximately 8,200,000 new returns are expected to be filed in 1941, and it is estimated that there were approximately 4,000,000 new taxpayers.

Although it leaves the personal exemptions unchanged, this bill will actually broaden the base. It makes the surtax applicable to the first dollar of income after the personal exemption and credit for dependents, and since the earned income credit is allowed for normal tax but not for surtax purposes, some income not now subject to tax will be subject to the surtax. Under existing law the earned income credit permits a single person to be free of income tax unless his income is in excess of $888, while a married couple with no dependents is free of income tax unless it receives more than $2,222, although the personal exemption in these instances are only $800 and $2,000, respectively. The result of the application of the surtax to the first dollar of surtax net income, as provided in this bill, is to make taxable approximately 2,470,000 people who otherwise would be free of tax with the same income. These, together with the persons who will become taxable as a result of increases in their income are expected to raise the number of 1942 income taxpayers 3,405,000 over the 1941 number.

It is estimated that if the pending bill is enacted, 17,107,000 individual income tax returns will be filed during the calendar year 1942. Of this number 10,925,000 will be taxable.

In the early stages of this bill the Treasury Department took the position that in view of this substantial broadening of the base personal exemptions should not be lowered further. However, the threat of rising prices alters the situation. If the cost of living rises substantially, the effect will be to tax small incomes much more than an income tax would at the rates provided in this bill. The reduction of personal exemptions will make it possible for a large number of persons in the country to feel that they are making direct contributions to the defense program. During the course of this tax bill we have had evidence that many people want to make such a direct contribution.

As the Secretary pointed out, persons with small incomes should have an opportunity for filing a short simple return and finding the amount of the tax on a table instead of being obliged to file the regular return and to make the regular tax computation. The Secretary has placed in your hands an illustrative schedule and discussed briefly its application.

I would like to indicate in somewhat more detail how the proposal would operate. It is intended to apply primarily to persons with income from wages, salaries and interest. A great majority of small incomes is of these types. The incomes of small businessmen, however, are more complicated, involving as they do costs of materials, inventories, depreciation and other expense items.

The simple return form would not be of value to them since computations of these items would be necessary before income could be determined. For other taxpayers with incomes of not more than $3,000, however, the short form would be provided.

Since the short form would be made optional rather than compulsory, the taxpayer would not lose any rights he has under existing law to benefit if he desires from specific deductions such as losses not covered by insurance or capital losses.

In order that the typical taxpayer using the simple table might derive substantially the same tax benefit from deductions that he now derives, the tax appearing on the table would take into account the average amount now deducted by persons with small incomes. Finally, in order to simplify the income tax table, incomes would be grouped in blocks of $25 with the same tax payable for all incomes within the block.

For example, take the case of a single man with a salary of $1880. If we assume that the personal exemptions recommended by the President of $750 for single persons and $1500 for married persons and heads of families were adopted, this taxpayer would compute his tax in the following manner:

On the face of the short income tax form he would write down his salary of $1880. He would then look on the back of the return and see that this income fell in the block from $1876 to $1900. He would find that this tax is $94 and this he would enter on the front of the return and pay that amount as his tax. Again, take the example of a married couple with two children having a salary income of $2700 and interest of $54, or a total of $2754. These two items of income and the total would be entered on the face of the return. Turning to the back of the return the taxpayer would subtract from the $2754, the credit of $800 for his two dependents. The remaining income would be $1954. He would look on the table and find that he owed a tax of $33.

It is thus seen that the computation of the tax would be extremely simple.

The estate tax changes in the bill are likewise limited to rate increases. The Treasury's recommendations that the $40,000 insurance exclusion under the estate tax and the $40,000 specific exemption under the estate and gift taxes be reduced to $25,000 each, were not incorporated in this bill. The increases in the estate tax rates in the bill extend throughout the rate schedule but are substantially lower than those proposed by the Treasury. The present two percent rate on the first bracket of the net estate has been increased to three percent. The maximum rate of 70 percent effective on the bracket in excess of $50,000,000 has been shifted to become effective on that portion of the net estate exceeding $10,000,000. The gift tax rates have also been increased so that they continue to be three-fourths of the estate tax rates. The anticipated revenue increase from these changes amounts to $151.9 million. It has been estimated that if the higher rates and lower exemptions proposed by the Treasury were adopted, the increased yield would be $347.2 million.

The pending bill makes several changes in the corporation taxes. It gives expression to the principle that corporations generally, even those without excessive profits, should bear part of the heavy burden imposed by the defense program. To that end, it provides for an increase in the corporation income tax of 5 percent on the first $25,000 of surtax net income and 6 percent on the balance. This increase—as that of the personal income tax—is imposed in the form of a surtax, in order to reach a substantial part of the interest from more than $20 billion of partially tax-exempt securities which are held by corporations, principally banks and insurance companies. Corporations having incomes over $25,000 will thus be taxed at an effective rate of almost 30 percent.

When these partially tax-exempt securities were issued, it was impossible to foresee the extraordinary demands which would be made upon the American people. Neither the Government nor the corporate purchasers anticipated that the tax benefit from these partially tax-exempt securities would be as great as it is. Each increase in the normal tax rate has increased the tax savings which accrue to the corporate holders of these bonds. To avoid granting a further unexpected bonus, it is necessary that the increase in rates be in the form of a surtax.

It has been pointed out, however, that the combined effect of this surtax, together with the postponement of deductions attributable to bonds purchased at a premium until the bonds mature or are sold, may adversely affect the market for many outstanding Treasury securities. I therefore suggest that consideration be given, in the case of public and private bonds purchased at a premium, to requiring the holder to amortize the premium over the life of the bond in place of the present system of allowing a capital loss at the time of maturity measured by the difference between purchase price and redemption price. Such a proposal would, in effect, treat the interest on such bonds at the effective rate rather than at the coupon rate for tax purposes and would thus be both more realistic and in accordance with commercial practice.

The bill makes permanent the defense taxes which were imposed for a five year period by the Revenue Act of 1940. These defense taxes amount, in general, to 10 percent of the taxes to which they are added. In view of their now permanent nature, I suggest that these defense tax rates be integrated with the other tax rates, so that the amount of the various taxes can be computed on the basis of a single rate structure. This will simplify both the text of the revenue laws and the computations to be made by taxpayers thereunder.

In the case of the capital stock tax, the House bill increases the tax rate from $1.10 to $1.25 upon each $1,000 of the declared value of capital stock. The anticipated gross increase in revenue from this change is $22.3 millions.

The proposed changes in the excess profits tax are estimated to increase the revenue from this tax by $1,198.3 million. This increase in revenue is accomplished without change in the optional methods of computing the excess profits credit provided by the Second Revenue Act of 1940. The Secretary has already called to your attention the fact that the department does not favor a continuation of a method which leaves free of excess profits tax those corporations with consistently high earnings which represent the greatest ability to pay.

The bill increases the rates of tax, modifies the excess profits tax base, and imposes a special tax on corporations using the invested capital credit.

The tax brackets of the existing law, graduated according to the amount of the adjusted excess profits net income, are retained. The increase in the tax rate amounts to 10 percentage points in each bracket. The proposed rates range from 35 percent on adjusted excess profits net income of not more than $20,000 to 60 percent on amounts over $500,000. The corresponding rates in the existing law are 25 percent and 50 percent.

The most important structural change provided by the bill is the disallowance of the income tax as a deduction in computing the excess profits tax. This change will increase the amount of income subject to the excess profits tax and hence the revenue from the excess profits tax. However, the increase will be partly offset by a decrease in the income subject to the corporation income tax because the excess profits tax is allowed as a deduction for the purpose of computing the income tax, both normal and surtax.

The excessiveness of profits should be measured by the whole of corporate profits as proposed in the bill and not by the part remaining after income tax as in the present law. Under graduated rates the present procedure results in dropping the taxable excess profits into the lower bracket rates, thus diminishing the revenue. Further, because the base period income tax is lower than the current income tax (16-1/2 percent as against 24 percent for 1940 and 30 percent for 1941) corporations using the average earnings method are allowed a greater deduction from profits of the current year than from the profits of the base period average. Such reduction in the excess profits tax of corporations using the average earnings methods seems entirely unwarranted in view of the already liberal excess profits credits.

In the existing law the invested capital credit is a flat 8 percent on the entire amount of the invested capital. The bill provides that the credit be reduced to 7 percent on invested capital exceeding $5,000,000.

In order not to discourage new equity financing, it is desirable to allow a larger tax-free return on new capital than would be obtainable under the reversal in method of computing the tax. A special allowance on new capital investment when the excess profits credit is computed under the invested capital method is made by including new capital at 125 percent of its value. This is the equivalent of allowing an invested capital credit with respect to new capital of 10 percent where the total invested capital is less than $5,000,000 and 8-3/4 percent where the invested capital is more than $5,000,000.

The allowance is applicable only on new capital which consists of money or property paid in for stock. It does not extend to new capital raised by borrowing nor to earnings and profits retained in the business. Safeguards are provided against the use of the new capital allowance for tax avoidance purposes.

The excess profits tax in the present law fails to reach a very large part of defense profits, despite the clear expression of Congressional intent that profits growing out of the defense effort should be subject to excess profits tax. Our examination of the available data shows that many corporations that are the principal beneficiaries of the defense effort and whose profits in 1940 were many times larger than in 1939 and in any of the preceding base period years will pay little or no excess profits tax. This situation cannot be justified in the light of the growing revenue requirements. In order to reach these profits which are attributable solely to the defense program, the Treasury recommended and the bill provides that a flat rate of 10 percent should be applied in such cases to that part of the current profits that exceeds the base period earnings but does not exceed the invested capital credit.

The excise portions of the pending bill are estimated to yield $874.8 millions. Forty-six percent of this total derives from raising the rates or broadening the bases of 14 existing excises. Twenty-two new excises are expected to yield 54 percent of the total.

The Treasury recommended but the bill does not contain increases in the existing rates of tax on gasoline, tobacco products and beer. The Treasury also recommended that the present tax on passenger automobiles be increased to 15 percent; the bill provides for an increase to only 7 percent. At the same time, the Treasury does not approve all the excises incorporated in the present bill. Particularly, it disapproves the proposed five dollar use tax on every motor vehicle.

This tax will conflict directly with one of the most important State and local sources of revenue. In some States the proposed tax will in effect increase the average cost of automobile registration by more than 100 percent.

The proposed tax has no relationship to the extent of use or value of the object taxed and, therefore, is unusually inequitable.

It taxes a $5,000 town car exactly the same $5 as the fifth-hand car worth only $20. This proposed use tax must be collected from 32,000,000 taxpayers located throughout every State and county in the country. This would require an additional personnel in the Bureau of Internal Revenue of at least 3,800. The administrative cost is estimated to be $9.6 millions or approximately $6 per $100 of tax collected, which is more than five times the average cost of collecting other excise taxes. This automobile use tax is estimated to yield about $160 millions. Contrast these figures with those pertaining, for example, to the gasoline tax. That tax, yielding $343 millions, is collected by 15 internal revenue employees. In this regard it should be noted that to the average motorist who travels 10,000 miles annually the use tax is equivalent in burden to a ½ cent gasoline tax. Or, contrast the proposed automobile use tax with the tobacco taxes. Their annual yield is $698 millions which is collected by 88 internal revenue employees. An increase in either the gasoline tax or the tobacco tax, moreover, would not require any additional personnel.

The measure before you will constitute the largest tax act in history. The Committee on Ways and Means has labored on it assiduously and conscientiously for the past 3-1/2 months. Some have criticized this bill as severe but our present national peril requires many sacrifices. The severity of this bill is minor when compared to the severity of other sacrifices which are cheerfully made by our citizens. At a time when many men are being called upon to forego gainful occupations to enter our armed forces for a remuneration of $21 per month and at a time when it has become necessary to extend their period of service, these citizens in civilian life will, I am sure, cheerfully make the contributions called for under this bill and will be ready to make even greater contributions if it becomes necessary.

APPENDIX C

Treasury Department
Washington
FOR RELEASE, MORNING NEWSPAPERS PRESS SERVICE
Tuesday, January 20, 1942.   No. 29-71

(The following address by Assistant Secretary of the Treasury John L. Sullivan before the biennial dinner for the incoming General Assembly of Virginia at the John Marshall Hotel, Richmond, Virginia, is scheduled for 8 p.m. Eastern Standard Time, Monday, January 19, 1942, and is for release upon delivery at that time.)

I am most grateful for the opportunity given to me to meet tonight with this distinguished group of the leaders of Virginia. A visit to Virginia, the home of the Presidents and the stage upon which much of America's most vital early drama was enacted, is always stimulating. During such a period as the present—when freedom throughout the world is in dire jeopardy—the memories of what Virginia has been and what Virginians have wrought are truly inspiring.

But the contribution of this Commonwealth is not restricted to the past, for today the sons of Virginia are adding new glories to your history, and in the councils of the Federal Government they maintain the prestige your representatives have always enjoyed. In Washington, Congressmen Bland, Harris, Satterfield, Drewry, Burch, Smith and Flannagan have again and again demonstrated their worthiness to carry on your great traditions. Congressman Woodrum, an outstanding leader in the House of Representatives, never fails to exert his very considerable influence toward the accomplishment of those objectives which wisdom and vision indicate are for the good of the nation. Congressman Robertson, a leading member of the House Ways and Means Committee, has proved invaluable in helping to solve some of the Government's most trying problems.

To the United States Senate Virginia has sent two statesmen. Harry Byrd has set a standard for frankness, intellectual honesty and courage that is so needed in these trying days. His early experience in the Virginia Senate, his four years as Governor of this Commonwealth, and his nine years as a member of the United States Senate, have given to his inquiring mind opportunities for intimate knowledge of the detailed affairs of Government. His acceptance of those opportunities has made him one of the Senate's ablest members.

Virginia claims another member of the Senate, but although he has always ably represented the interests of his own Commonwealth and of his own constituents, I challenge Virginia's claim upon him. For the last forty-two years as a member of the Virginia Senate, the National House of Representatives, as Secretary of the Treasury, and as a member of the United States Senate, he has devoted himself to the service of his country. His accomplishments challenge the record of his contemporaries. As the father of the Federal Reserve System he brought stability to commerce and to private banking, and won for the nation fiscal security. He's a thinker, and he's a fighter, too. As such he is respected, appreciated and loved throughout the land. Though he was born in Lynchburg, and has always been elected by Virginians, I say he belongs to all America. He is America's Senator at Large, Carter Glass.

It is a great privilege for me to be here with you tonight on this particular occasion. Here with us are gathered the recently elected members of the General Assembly, who on Wednesday, as free representatives of free people, will meet to construct the framework of restrictions within which the men and women of Virginia can conduct themselves in war time and still be free. In how very few places in the world are people now allowed to regulate and restrain themselves through restrictions they impose upon themselves! In the deliberations of the General Assembly, the members are free and equal agents; free to thin, speak, act and vote as they chose—answerable only to their constituents and to their own consciences. We who have so long taken this for granted are apt to forget how much this means to us, until we stop to remember the liberty lost and the freedom strangled in the last three years in Austria, Czecholavakia, Poland, Denmark, Norway, Luxembourg, Holland, Belgium, France, Bulgaria, Yugolslavia, Albania and Greece.

Surely now is the time for America's torch of liberty and freedom to burn brightly to show to the oppressed peoples of the world the path back to freedom, Democracy and enlightened civilization. This is the time for Democracy and for you, its representatives, to do even better than your best. You succeed men who have set a standard for you. I wish to congratulate Governor Price and his associates upon their fine administration, and I extend to Governor-elect Darden and to you his colleagues best wishes for an administration worthy of Virginia's rich heritage. Much is at stake, for you represent the values of living Democracy.

I have been asked to speak tonight on the role of Federal Taxation in this time of war. I doubt if any field of legislation Democracy is better exemplified than in taxation. In some quarters there appears to be a feeling that Federal taxes are a vial type of oppression, brewed by the Treasury alchemist during the dark of the moon, and forced through Congress upon a reluctant populace. Having chaperoned five tax bills through Congress, I can tell you that nothing could be further from the truth.

Long before the Republic was born we had set ideas about taxation without representation. Though such a threat has long since disappeared, the hostility to it remains, and today in America taxes are imposed upon the people by the people themselves, who acting through their own representatives determine what burden they shall assume for the national good. Probably in no phase of any type of Government in the world today does Government depend more directly upon the consent of the governed than in the field of American Federal taxes. Under the Constitution Federal Taxes can originate in one place and in one place only,--the House of Representatives. As the Department charged with the administration and collection of taxes, the Treasury is called upon to consult with and to advise the Congress. When requested, the Treasury presses its views. But the Treasury never, never writes a tax bill. The Congress does that.

It might be well at this time, when the democratic processes are under fire for me to tell you a bit about how this works out. I doubt very much if the average American citizen has any appreciation of how long and how hard the Congress works on our tax problems.

A tax bill originates in the House Ways and Means Committee, when the Secretary of the Treasury and his fiscal assistants are invited to appear at a public hearing to submit such proposals and observations as they deem worthy of Congressional consideration. These hearings,--and the later hearings before the Senate Finance Committee, are largely attended and widely publicized. Usually at the opening session there are batteries of newsreel cameras and scores of reporters. While the cameras grind and the journalists scribble out tomorrow's headlines, it is quite natural that the non-administration members should go after the witnesses on a partisan basis,--though no more partisan than the manner in which the administration members rush to the defense of their administration.

The public hearings end, and the Committees go into Executive Sessions. Coats come off, sleeves are rolled up and the Committee members get down to work, not as fifteen Democrats and ten Republicans, but as twenty-five sincere, conscientious public servants. I have yet to see but one partisan vote by either committee. I have never known any group in private industry to work as intensely or as long hours as these two committees. These Executive Sessions last for weeks and even temporary absence is a rarity. I can testify to the home work the committee do at night because of the number of calls I get through the evening, asking for additional information on some subject discussed during the day.

Surely the American taxpayer is safe in the hands of the House Ways and Means and the Senate Finance Committees and the Congress. Truly do they vindicate Democracy.

The magnitude of the task these two Committees and the Congress now face is unparalleled. That you may view it in its proper proportions may I give you some recent fiscal history:

In the year 1940,   7,600,000 income tax returns were filed.

In the year 1941,   15,200,000 income tax returns were filed.

In the year 1942,   22,000,000 income tax returns will be filed.

In the fiscal year 1940 the total gross tax yield was $5,303,000,000.

In the fiscal year 1941 the total gross tax yield was $7,361,000,000.

In the fiscal year 1942 the total gross tax yield is expected to reach $12,200,000,000.

In the fiscal year 1943 on the basis of present law we anticipate a yield of $17,261,000,000.

Thus from 1940 to 1943 not only have our tax receipts been trebled but the number of individual income tax filers has also been trebled. But are these collections adequate for the task we now face? Unfortunately they are not.

For the fiscal year 1943—the year during which we anticipate existing taxes to yield $18 billion—we expect to spend on the war alone $56 billion. This will exceed the total Federal expenditures for all purposes during the six years from 1935 through 1940. The need to pay as we go for a larger proportion of this expenditure resulted in the recommendation of the President that additional taxes and Social Security contributions be levied to yield $9 billion more a year. Better than words do these figures describe the task awaiting Congress.

The role of tax policy during this period is to become the servant of the war effort. This war is being fought with men and machines, with airplanes and ships, with guns and tanks,—not with dollars, not with taxes. A good fiscal policy alone cannot win this war no matter how many dollars it brings into the Treasury. A poor fiscal policy, however, can lose this war, or cause want and misery after the victory.

The primary purpose of ne taxes is to raise revenue, to meet a larger proportion of our current expenditures with current receipts, and thus to reduce the amount of borrowing that would otherwise be required. As we approach the largest national income any country in the world has ever achieved it would be folly indeed not to take a larger share of that income to pay our bills.

The American people know what is at stake today, and they know that no price can be too high for those precious freedoms we are defending. They know that if we are to preserve our American system we shall pay for every last gun and plane 100 cents on the dollar. They know, too, that every dollar paid in taxes this year saves at least another dollar in interest charges over the next 30 years—for they learned in the last war that interest costs will in time equal the original expenditures. So too do they know that taxes are the only source of revenue of our government—the only means of paying for what we buy or of repaying the money we borrow.

Obviously in taxes there is a point beyond which we cannot go without deadening individual initiative, dulling corporate management, encouraging extravagance and inefficiency and thus not only retarding our war effort but killing the goose that lays the golden egg. To approach—but not to reach—that point should be the major objective of the Congress in the next revenue bill.

But there are collateral objectives. This revenue bill should seek to preserve morale by distributing the tax burden equitably and with every regard for the ability to pay. It should wherever possible and wherever needed encourage the diversion of materials, equioment and skilled labor from civilian to war production. And above all it must be so devised that it will serve as a formidable weapon to combat inflation.

I am inclined to doubt that the average person in this country is yet aware of the imminent threat of inflation or the havoc it creates. Caused by an increase in the national purchasing power at the very time when our war effort requires us to reduce the production of goods for civilian consumption, it must inevitably start the cost of living in an upward spiral unless we can increase the production of civilian goods, or absorb some of the people's excess purchasing power. Since we cannot do the former without harm to our war effort we must do the latter. This we shall do by increased taxation and through the sale of Defense Bonds.

Now I realize that no one really enjoys paying increased taxes. But what is the alternative? During the last twelve months the cost of living has risen more than ten percent. For the great majority of the workers of this country that was exactly the same as though there had been a gross payroll tax of ten percent. Yet the huge sum such a tax would have yielded has vanished in the thin air of inflation—it has not bought one tank, one truck, or one revolver. Though cruelly hurting the wage earner it has not netted the Treasury one dollar, for the higher prices have materially increased the cost of all those things the Government must buy.

Having Uncle Sam as a partner in sharing the salary check or the wage envelope is far better than having the spectra of inflation as a guest at the dinner table. Tax increases are manageable by both Government and taxpayer. Each can see what is happening. The taxpayer can budget his resources and plan his spending with a reasonable degree of certainty. But he is defenseless before the creeping paralysis of inflation. How can he budget his resources when he does not know how much he must spend for eggs today, for eggs tomorrow, for eggs the day after, for butter, for bread?

Tax sacrifices are accompanied by an understanding of the contribution that is being made, by a realization that one is doing one's part in a bitter struggle. But the sacrifices of inflation are accompanied only by the fear of uncertainty, by the helplessness and the hopelessness that comes with trying to fight the invisible. Knowing all this, how far are we willing to go to prevent inflation? How deeply shall we ask the surgeon to cut to free us of this malignant growth?

The willingness of the American people to submit to substantially higher taxes is attested on all sides. The taxes which have been and will be imposed upon the American people have been imposed and will be voted by the duly elected representatives of the American people. The people of America know you cannot place a price tag on the freedom of speech. They know that no sum is too great to pay for freedom of worship. They know that freedom from want and freedom from fear are beyond evaluation.

They are willing to pay what must be paid—and to forego all those things needed for our armed forces. Without much flag waving but with a grim, realistic appraisal of the job that lies ahead, they await the leadership of the Administration and of the Congress to tell them what they must do to save America. That they will do.

We are going to win this war. We can't win it quickly; we can't win it easily, but win it we shall. We have the resources, the men and the machines. Of far greater importance we have the determination, for we all realize that we are fighting for more than a few islands in the Pacific, for more than free access to rubber, tin, and hemp, for more than free markets for our goods, or the maintenance of our standard of living. Our stake is freedom itself—individual equality and opportunity, the right of the human soul to expand and develop--the dignity of man.

Then when we have won this war,—God grant that under America's unselfish leadership the world may be led along the path of permanent peace. That is our task. That is America's destiny. To that, this nation is pledged. To that we dedicate ourselves.

APPENDIX D

Treasury Department
Washington

FOR RELEASE, MORNING NEWSPAPERS,   Press Service
<u>Monday, June 15, 1942.</u>   No. 32-5
6/12/42

(The following address by Assistant Secretary of the Treasury John L. Sullivan, before the United Nations Flag Day rally in Chicago, Illinois, is scheduled for delivery at <u>2 p.m. Central War Time, Sunday, June 14, 1942, and is for release at that time.</u>)

I am very happy to join with you folks today in celebrating Flag Day, and United Nations Day and in paying tribute to those gallant Americans who in distant lands are fighting under the leadership of one we honor today—General Douglas MacArthur. It was a stroke of genius to combine Flag Day and United Nations Day. I believe the same spirit out of which Flag Day arose and which made America a home of Liberty and a fortress of Freedom exists again today. That spirit is casting its influence over the widened horizons of a shrinking world. It gives promise to the United Nations and to all men of good will of an era of liberty, peace, and progress.

One hundred sixty-five years ago today, on the 14th of June, 1777, the Continental Congress selected as the banner of this new Republic the first model of that flag we love so well. That flag has since become for all the world the symbol of justice and fair play. Pause a moment and consider the gallantry and the faith of the men and women who made the Stars and Stripes possible. Thirteen handfuls of pioneers in isolated outposts. They didn't know each other very well; they had never relied on each other very much. Each colony had its own government, its own militia, its own special problems and interests. Communication among them hardly existed, and transportation was most difficult. It took ten days to make the journey fro Boston, to Philadelphia that we now make by plane in an hour and a half. Then the journey from New

Hampshire to Georgia took ten times as long as it takes today to fly to Australia and back. The colonists were a band of friendly strangers, facing the armed might of a greater military power. They were impoverished in all save the spirit and the courage to seek a pattern of life never before known and to establish a land where mankind could live truly free and truly equal.

We know what they suffered, from Lexington through Yorktown. We remember their hunger, their misery, their gallant deaths. We now know the value of every sacrifice they made, for they established Democracy in a land where it could and did achieve Freedom, Liberty and Equality. And this great nation today is a monument to those valiant men and women, men and women who really believed in the brotherhood of man. They saw a vision of a better life and they dared to die to make that dream come true.

Today the civilized world faces the same opportunity America faced 165 years ago. True, it is composed of geographically isolated nations, of differing races and creeds and tongues. But in terms of transportation and communication all the nations of the earth are closer to each other today than the thirteen colonies were. And during the last few years, America, yes, and Britain and Russia and China and a host of conquered nations have learned a lesson it took America eighty years to learn. Eighty-five years ago this week, speaking in Springfield, Abraham Lincoln declared that this nation could not endure half slave and half free. Today you and I and thoughtful people all over the world know that civilization itself cannot endure in a world half slave and half free. We know that on this shrinking globe the dwelling place of Freedom is the world itself. We know now that if Freedom is endangered anywhere it is in peril everywhere. We know that what the Chinese do today to the Japs in Chekiang, or the British do to Rommell in Lybia, or the Russians do to the Nazis at Kharkov will have a more direct and a more immediate effect on all of us than the Battle of Bunker Hill had on the Colonists of Virginia and the Carolinas. At long last we have learned how false is the security of isolation.

And so it is that America and the twenty-six other United Nations whose flags fly above you today have joined together, just as the thirteen colonies did, in a campaign of mutual helpfulness to defend our common liberties.

Here's what we propose to do:

We propose to preserve for ourselves and our children the freedom and the opportunity which we Americans have created in this nation.

We propose to help the nations allied with us to defend their threatened independence.

And we propose to restore the liberty which has been trampled and defiled and stolen from the lands of our ancestors—to bring freedom again to the people of Holland and Belgium—Poland and Norway and Denmark—to China and France and Czechoslovakia—to Greece, and the Ukraine,—to Albania and Yugoslavia—to all the beaten and broken but unconquered countries.

And here's how we Americans propose to do this:

We will build and man a Navy that will sink our enemies' ships beneath all of the seven seas.

We will build and man an air force that will sweep the world's skies clear.

We will man and equip armies that will crush the Nazis and Japs in Europe and Asia and Africa or wherever we have to chase them.

We will smash their war machines until there isn't enough left to sell for junk.

We will crush them so completely that they will never again dare to lift their hands against the free American people.

That is our plan for overwhelming the enemies of our nation and of all free people, and these are the ways we will accomplish that plan.

Every man who is fit and of an age to fight must fight. The Navy is asking Chicago for 10,000 volunteers. The Navy will get them. The Army Air Force is calling for men to fly its planes, and to service them, and to do ground work that will release flyers and fighters for active service. These are opportunities for those of us who are young enough and fit enough for active service, to do our part in this common struggle.

Many of us who cannot actually fight can still serve actively and vitally by <u>making</u> the weapons of our victory—the tanks and planes, the guns and ships, that will outshoot and overpower the enemy. They also serve who make the steel, and tend the lathes, and assemble the sinews of war. As new millions of citizens join the armed forces, as new munitions plants swing into production, millions more of our women and middle-aged men will find this their way of serving America. And this work must go forward without delay or interruption, as faithfully and continuously as the soldiers and sailors themselves serve.

And finally, all the rest of us, the millions of the civilian population, every man, woman and child, can and must serve the nation by lending our dollars. We must enlist them in our country's war effort—every last dollar we can spare—and many a dollar that we cannot spare.

We must enlist those dollars to buy the tanks and planes and guns to batter our enemies—dollars for ships—dollars to feed and clothe and pay our soldiers and sailors—dollars, billions of them to get our war effort into high gear and to keep it rolling in high gear.

The nation demands of its sailors and soldiers one hundred percent of all they have, even unto their very lives. The nation expects of the workers in its shipyards and munitions factories one hundred percent of their work and ability. Now the nation is asking of its people—all its people—that they set aside at least ten percent of all their income to pay for the things needed to wage this war to a successful finish. It asks at least a dime out of every dollar—a dollar out of every ten, to buy the War Bonds that will buy the planes and guns and tanks and ships our fighting men must have.

Our record of War Bond purchases is a record to be proud of. But good as it is, it is not yet good enough. Our national production for war has grown so greatly and so fast that our war expenditures now amount to four billion dollars a month. A large part of that staggering amount must be raised by War Bond purchases—purchases every pay day by you and me, and every loyal American. We must literally buy Bonds until it hurts. We—you and I—must provide the money to win this war. You know that there's no sense in building a bridge three-fourths of the way across a river. We must build the Bridge of Bonds <u>all</u> the way across, to carry our men and our weapons to victory.

To do this will mean buying Bonds first—bonds instead of luxuries; bonds instead of vacations; bonds instead of pleasures; bonds instead of scores of things we Americans have been used to buying. And I ask you to remember, when you start to buy some article which you do not really need, that you are actually depriving a soldier or sailor or aviator, of that much equipment or arms or ammunition—or some civilian war worker of an article which might have made him or her a more productive worker for our common cause.

Money which you invest in War Bonds is not money spent but money saved. The bonds you buy are the finest, strongest securities in the world. They are backed with the entire resources and strength of the United States Government. They increase in value as you hold them so that when they come to maturity you will receive $4 back for every $3 you spent for them.

In the meanwhile you cannot lode a penny—because United States War Savings Bonds have a guaranteed value, at all times, of at least the full price you paid for them.

And all the time they give you an ever-increasing fund of savings to fall back upon when you need it, and to plan a secure future for your family.

The people of Chicago and of Illinois are to be congratulated upon their splendid response to our War Savings Bonds appeal. Your record ranks high among the cities and states of the nation. But the fact remains that more—far more War Bonds must be purchased and at a greatly accelerated pace. I am confident that the Treasury can rely upon you. You know what is at stake. You know that no one can place a price tag on the freedom of speech. You know that no sum is too great to pay for freedom of worship. You know that freedom from want and freedom from fear are beyond evaluation. And I know you will scrimp and save to protect those priceless freedoms.

This will be a hard war. It may be a long war. No one can foretell just when or how it will end. But of this much I am sure: Whether it lasts one year or five, those years will see America at her best. There is a spirit abroad in this land today that lifts men and women above themselves. Literally millions of our people who have never before shown any great interest in public affairs or the activities of their own communities are today willingly and proudly giving their time and work to a gallant purpose. They are taking first aid courses, they are selling War Bonds, they are training in hospitals as nurses aides, they are driving trucks and ambulances. They are sitting up half the night every night as airplane spotters and wardens. Without pay they are doing the hard, dirty, thankless jobs that this new kind of war inflicts upon a people. And for most of them these thankless jobs have become the most important thing in their lives.

Here in Chicago as everywhere in the country, it is an inspiration to see how our people have rallied to those unaccustomed tasks and how well they are doing them. It is a convincing demonstration of democracy at work, and it carries with it a promise of great things for the future. These millions of new unselfish public servants must not lose their interest in public affairs and retire into their former seclusion when this war ends. I don't think they will. I think this awakening of the democratic processes will mean a revitalized America. So too will the voice of these millions be heard at the peace tables.

All of us in America today would gladly give our lives to prevent a repetition of what we are now going through. A single generation that knew not only Chateau Thierry, Belleau Woods, Soissons and the Argonne but also knew Pearl Harbor, Bataan, Wake and Guam—we know what war means—and we know the misery that follows a war. We don't shrink from war. But we do recoil from the stupidity of a bungling peace that begets more wars and breeds more misery. I think I speak the mind of the United Nations and I know I speak the mind of America when I say that this war must end with a just and enduring peace. It must not happen again. This nation and our allies must build a world of international peace and progress that will endure for generations. To this we dedicate ourselves today. This we shall achieve, God willing, under the leadership of one of the greatest friends and leaders humanity has ever known—Franklin Delano Roosevelt.

APPENDIX E

16 February 1949

STATEMENT OF THE SECRETARY OF THE NAVY
BEFORE THE SUBCOMMITEE OF THE HOUSE
APPROPRIATIONS COMMITTEE
IN CONNECTION WITH APPROPRIATION ESTIMATES OF
THE DEPARTMENT OF THE NAVY FOR FISCAL YEAR 1950

I am very happy to have this opportunity to meet with the members of this subcommittee and to discuss the appropriation estimates of the Department of the Navy for the fiscal year 1950. I intend to make my observations rather general in character and leave the detailed testimony for subsequent witnesses.

President Truman's budget, now before you, allocates to the Navy a total of four billion, 347 million in new obligating authority. Though the total proposed appropriations for the Navy are 600 million dollars less than the naval appropriations for the current fiscal year, the Navy accepts and completely supports President Truman's budget.

The smaller amount proposed for the fiscal year 1950 will, of course, finance a lesser degree of Naval activity than is now possible with the current funds. The Navy considers this reduces scale of activity to be the minimum acceptable. We accept it because of the over-riding necessity for a military budget consistent with the needs of our national economy which is the indispensable basis of all our military strength. In the light of present and foreseeable world conditions, however, reductions on the immediate readiness of the active fleet below the levels contemplated by the proposed budget would project calculated naval risks beyond reasonable limits.

I scarcely need remind the members of this Committee that we do not yet live in a peaceful world. We have still before us many problems to be settled before the peace treaties with Germany, Austria and Japan can be negotiated and presented to the Senate for ratification. The United Nations still lacks the means to implement its international police functions. Despite the large scale contributions of food, money and other assistance which this nation has freely made, and is making, to troubled countries throughout the world there still exists widespread hunger, fear and misery in many areas. Such conditions breed political turmoil and unrest.

One important peacetime function of our Navy in these troubled times is to further the interests of peace and stability by its mere presence in waters contiguous to troubled areas. It is the only one of our armed forces, symbolic of the power and might of the United States, and whose movements are sanctioned by international custom and tradition, that can patrol the sea lanes of the earth, and act not merely as our watch-dogs but also as ambassadors of good will. On such peaceful errands our ships and naval aircrafts serve as a very real and visible symbol of democratic strength.

As we survey our new position of world leadership we are necessarily mindful of the tremendous responsibilities which we must assume. We face a world situation which calls for broader decisions than any in our past history. We have few procedures upon which we can rely for guidance. In heeding the cries of humanity we have committed this nation to a course of assistance to bolster the economy of those nations who struggle to retain their independence. By such steps we hope in time to develop a state of stability and harmony among nations which will permit a relaxation of armaments, allowing men to devote their major energies to the productions of instruments of better living rather than to the maintenance of large military forces. Yet, until the minimum conditions for satisfactory international agreements have been met we cannot discard our weapons, desert our responsibility, and leave in jeopardy our far-flung occupation forces overseas.

We Americans do not usually think of ourselves as a "have-not nation" but we must face the fact that in many strategic raw materials we are woefully far from being self-sufficient. Little does the average man realize to what extent his daily livelihood and well-being—in many instances, even his job—are dependent upon the uninterrupted flow of such critical materials from overseas. I think manganese from India and Africa, around the Cape of Good Hope and across the Atlantic; of tin from Malaya; and of chromite from Africa and Asia. Without these vital imports our national economy as we know it could not long survive. For as many years ahead as we can see these cargoes will come to us in ocean-going vessels. The protection of these cargoes—the maintenance of these open sea lanes—continues, as always in the past, to be the basic function of sea power. In peacetime our prosperity would be crippled without the steady intake of essential imports through the pipe lines of our ocean commerce. In wartime, unless those pipe lines of critical raw materials could be expanded without serious interruption, our war effort would be feeble and short-lived. We intend that within the screen of naval power, if need be, and under the umbrella of air protections, those cargoes will always be able to move.

In short, these considerations explain in part why we cannot abandon our naval strength, and why we cannot predicate our naval needs on a mere relative comparison with the navies of other powers.

In the preparation of the 1950 budget a determined effort was made within the National Military Establishment, under the direction of the Secretary of Defense, to correlate the budgets of that Establishment for the first time under the National Security Act. Months were spent by the Joint Chiefs of Staff and their assistants in analyzing the initial budget submission of the three Departments.

The Joint Chiefs of Staff, with the approval of the Secretary of Defense, set the amount allocated to the Department of the Navy under the ceiling of 15 billion dollars for the National Military Establishment was 4 billion 624 million dollars in new obligating authority. After review by the Bureau of the Budget, the amount contained in the President's budget for the Navy, now before you, is 4 billion 347 million dollars in new obligating authority. A portion of this difference represents a reserve to provide obligating authority for legislative items not yet authorized by the Congress.

Operating Forces

In appearing before the Congress in the supplemental appropriations for fiscal year 1949, I indicated the forces which would be maintained during the current fiscal year. Plans for operation forces in fiscal 1950, which support the budget estimates now before you, showed that immediate revision of our 1949 plans was necessary. These changes were of such magnitude that it was found necessary to commence an orderly phasing into the 1950 plans as early as possible so that the maximum force could be maintained throughout that year. It is for this reason that we have determined to reduce our forces in an orderly manner during the remainder of fiscal 1949.

I had hoped to acquaint this Committee in regular budget hearings of the necessity for retrenchment before any conclusive action was taken in this regard. My letter to you of February 2 was sent because early action was indicated, and a definite date for commencement of hearings had not been determined.

The request now before you provides an average of 472,00 <u>regular</u> personnel of the Navy and Marine Corps in fiscal 1950. This is a reduction of 29,000 below the 501,000 on board as of 31 December 1948.

In addition, provision is made for the 36,000 one-year enlistees, provided by the Selective Service Act of 1948, together with reservists on duties in connection with Reserve training and other trainees, which increases the average to 527,000 in 1950.

In terms of operating ships, to achieve the most efficient and economical transition to the fiscal year 1950 position, and to reduce diversion from the operation forces of personnel needed for inactivations to the minimum practicable, a program of inactivations has been prepared and integrated with the schedule of newly constructed and converted ships joining the Fleet during the fiscal year 1950.

With respect to the principal combatant types, 8 attack carriers will be active during fiscal 1950 instead of the 11 now being operated; 18 cruisers instead of 26 now being operated; and 170 destroyer types will be assigned to the Active Fleets compared to the 147 now being operated. The number of submarines in commission will be increased by 2. These changes, plus inactivations of other types, result in a net reduction from the present Active Fleet strength of 755 vessels to a total strength of 731.

Plans for 1950 provide 5582 operating aircraft for the Regular Navy and 2183 for the Navy and Marine Corps Air

Reserve, a total of 7765. This is another area in which immediate revision of 1949 plans, which provide for 10,687 operating aircrafts by 30 June 1949, was required.

Other witnesses will present our aircraft program in greater detail but I should like to point out that the rate of modernization of our aircrafts contemplated in the 1950 budget is considerable the standard required to maintain this force in "first line" condition.

Naval and Marine Corps Reserve

As the members of the Committee know, the Navy recognizes that a large and well trained Reserve is essential to real preparedness. Conscious of this necessity, the Naval and Marine Corps Reserves are administered and operated as an integral part of the Naval Establishment. The Committee will note during the course of the hearings which follow that each Chief of Bureau will have contained in his respective appropriations separate projects which indicate his proportion of the total funds allocated for Reserve programs. Plans for 1950 call for a total Naval Reserve of 1,415,000 personnel whom an average of 230,220 will be in organized drill pay status. This is an increase of 240,000 personnel in the total and 34,403 in the average number in organized drill pay status. For the Marine Corps, plans contemplate a total of 161,000 during 1950 of whom and average of 50,772 will be in organized drill pay status. This is an increase of 21,805 in the total number and 13,211 in drill pay status over current fiscal year plans.

At this time there are 269 Training Centers in use by the Surface Naval Reserve. By 30 June this year it is expected that a total of 317 Training Centers will be in use; an additional 5 are scheduled for completion during fiscal 1950. This will complete the current program of Naval Reserve Training Centers. In addition, 171 ships are berthed at appropriate locations for use in Naval Reserve Training.

For training of the Marine Corps Reserve, 52 Training Centers are now in use; in addition, members of the Marine Corps Reserve share 55 Naval Reserve Training Centers.

The air components of the Navy and Marine Corps Reserve utilize 23 Air Stations, and have assigned for training 2183 airplanes and 2 operation lighter-than-air ships.

Shipbuilding Program

The 1950 Shipbuilding program provides for the construction of 1 prototype motor minesweeper and for the conversion of 6 destroyers to destroyer escorts with improved antisubmarine warfare characteristics. There is included in the budget 52 million, 300 thousand dollars in obligating authority for this program.

This program represents a substantial reduction below that authorized for fiscal 1949 under which the construction of 5 new ships and the conversion of 17 others were authorized. Because of the time required to design and construct ships, there is considerable time lag between the preparation of estimates and the obligation and expenditure of funds. For example, estimates for the Shipbuilding program for fiscal 1949 were based on price levels as of August 1947 obligations could not be entered into until after 1 July 1948. As you know, ships require several years to build after the contract has been placed; expenditures for construction of ships authorized for fiscal 1948 will continue, in some cases, through fiscal 1952. Needless to say, difficulties arise in estimating the expenditure of funds so far in advance for ship construction due to sizable fluctuation in costs of labor and material.

Because of these price changes it has been necessary to re-estimate the cost of shipbuilding programs previously authorized. It is largely because of this increase that the 1950 program has been held to $52 million rather than the $225 million recommended by the Joint Chiefs of Staff.

In connection with the Shipbuilding program, I am sure the Committee is interested in the effect of the Navy Shipbuilding program upon the steel industry. Current estimates are, according to my understanding, that the total production of steel of all types in calendar year 1949 is estimated at 87,000,000 tons. The total Navy use for all purposes in calendar year 1949, including shipbuilding, is approximately 438,000 tons of ½ of 1 per cent of the total steel production.

Between now and the beginning of fiscal 1950, plans are under way to deactivate 9 Naval Air Stations, as indicated to you in my letter of February 2. The possibility of making additional reductions in the Shore Establishment is under continuous study.

The Secretary of Defense has discussed with you the joint use of facilities within the National Military Establishment. I should like to emphasize that I am heartily in accord with this program and the Navy is cooperating in every way therewith.

Research and Development

All Research and Development items included in the Navy budget have been approved by the Research and Development Board. For fiscal year 1950 our budget is for $203 million of new obligating authority compared with $233 million appropriated in the fiscal year 1949. Because of the great importance which technological improvements bear to the effectiveness of striking forces, we believe that the maintenance of a high level of activity and effort in this field is vital.

Material Readiness

Admiral Denfeld will inform you of the state of material readiness of the fleet. Funds now available and contemplated for 1950 for ship maintenance of budgetary limitations during the past several years, modernization of ships and aircraft, to keep pace with current developments has, of necessity, been at a much lower level than I would like to see. The status of maintenance of the Shore Establishments is important to the support of the fleet. Those Shore Establishments which remain active are being maintained at such minimum standards that we are not even holding our own against deterioration of many structures.

The Navy continues to emphasize and place in high priority the program of identification, segregation, and preservation of "roll-back" material left over from the war.

The Navy Cataloging program which provides for standardization of class description and stock numbers will be approximately 50 per cent completed by the end of the current fiscal year; completion is estimated as June 1952. The Navy program in his field is keyed in with and part of the program of the Munitions Board for the National Military Establishment.

Public Quarters

I feel that I must advise the Committee of the effects of one of the General Provisions, No. 113, now contained in the budget for the Navy. For purpose of ready reference I quote this provision as follows:

"SEC. 113. After June 30, 1949, no appropriation contained in this or any other Act shall be available for payment of rental of quarters allowances to personnel of the Services mentioned in the title of the Pay Readjustment act of 1942 for any periods during which the occupy, with their dependents, if any, quarters under the jurisdiction (for rental purposes) of any such services."

In view of the general critical shortage of housing during the way and the immediate post-war period, the Navy acquired from other Federal agencies a large number of units of defense housing located in the vicinity of naval activities. Most of these units are below the standards prescribed for permanent public quarters and consist of Quonset huts, trailers, converted temporary buildings, and low cost defense housing which are substandard as to construction and size. By this means both the Navy and the respective communities benefitted.

Since these housing units were not specifically constructed or designated for occupancy as public quarters, personnel who occupied these temporary quarters were required to pay rent at rates in keeping with local rentals rather than lose those entire amount of rental allowance provided under the Pay Readjustment Act. This was done in accordance with authority contained in Public Law 120 (79th Congress). The size of this housing varies from 200 square feet in trailers to 790 square feet in emergency housing; the size of public quarters now authorized by law varies from 1080 square feet for enlisted personnel to 2100 square feet for flag officers.

Presently 19,776 enlisted and 5,667 officers occupy this emergency housing and will, if the General Provision under discussion enacted, be deprived of their rental allowances, even though the housing in not considered adequate. I feel that this is a very unsatisfactory situation.

In conclusion, the appropriations which the Navy requests as part of President Truman's budget will maintain the minimum active naval power consistent with our national needs, prevent the obsolescence of that naval power by moderate construction, research and development programs, and train the numbers of personnel essential for the active reserve fleets. The funds which we seek will furnish the minimum Navy able in these times to support the traditional military policy of the United Sates. That policy is as it has always been, that the United States seeks no territory, wants no conflict, but if attacked, will do everything in its power to see that the resultant combat will be fought as far away as possible. Our Navy today is keeping station in waters far off our shores. In the event of any emergency, our naval forces in far waters would be among those who would give a good account of themselves in the first attacks and would do everything possible to keep those attacks from penetrating to our homeland. That is one of the fundamental missions of our Navy. That is the purpose for which we seek funds to maintain the minimum Navy capable of accomplishing that mission.

Index

Acknowledgments

This book could never have been written without the cooperation of the Sullivan family—John L.'s three children, Patricia, Charles, and Deborah. Pat, a history buff who has held on to many old photographs, news clippings, and books saved by her mother, was particularly helpful and enthusiastic about the project.

Because of the present unavailability of many government records, I have relied upon secondary material in certain areas. Paolo Coletta's 1981 fine history, *The United States Navy and Defense Unification, 1947–1953*, was particularly helpful in this regard.

Peter Gelfan at The Editorial Department provided first-rate critiques and editing.

I received invaluable suggestions from friends, including John Borgia, Roy Bowman, Doug Fisher, Chuck Bowsher and Jim Wade. Admiral Bruce Demars helped in getting data from the United States Navy; and Bill Scott provided needed information on the Marine Corps. Bill Geoghegan and Bud Vieth gave me strong encouragement.

Thanks to Connie Fields for the account of the dinner at Governor Fuller's home, to the gracious and helpful staffs at the Truman and FDR libraries, at Dartmouth's Rauner Special Collections Library, to Eileen O'Brien, curator of Library Collections at the Manchester Historic Association, and to Sally Fellows, archives and records manager, City of Manchester, New Hampshire.

I am grateful for the support and excellent product of my fine publisher, Deidre Randall and her staff at Peter E. Randall Publisher, and Grace Peirce's book design.

Throughout the process, my wife, Mary Claire, was a stalwart, reviewing, editing, solving computer problems, and pulling me away from my desk to eat and rest. Thank you again, my love.

About the Author

STEPHEN CLARKSON is a graduate of Yale College and the University of Virginia School of Law. He practiced law in New York City and Washington, D.C., where he was Secretary Sullivan's law partner from 1969 to 1982. He later became vice president, general counsel, and secretary of Newport News Shipbuilding in Virginia. Now retired, he and his wife, Mary Claire, live in Rye Beach, New Hampshire. He has previously published an historical novel, *Patriot's Reward*, the part-factual, part-fictional story of a slave owned by his ancestors in Portsmouth, New Hampshire, during the American Revolution.